CHRISTIAN RESEARCHES IN ASIA

CHRISTIAN RESEARCHES IN ASIA;

With Notices

OF THE

TRANSLATION OF THE SCRIPTURES

INTO

THE ORIENTAL LANGUAGES.

CLAUDIUS BUCHANAN, D.D.

GYAN

Published by

Gyan Publishing House
5, Ansari Road
Daryaganj, New Delhi-110002
Phone: 011-47034999, 9811692060
E-mail: books@gyanbooks.com

Distribution Network
gyanbooks.com
India, USA, Canada, UK, Australia, France

ISBN: 978-81-212-9418-8 (PB)
First Published, 1811

2nd Impression 2023

Printed at: Gyan Press, Delhi.

CHRISTIAN RESEARCHES IN ASIA
AUTHOR: CLAUDIUS BUCHANAN

CHRISTIAN

RESEARCHES IN ASIA;

With Notices

OF THE

TRANSLATION OF THE SCRIPTURES

INTO

THE ORIENTAL LANGUAGES.

"And I saw another Angel fly in the midst of heaven, having the EVERLASTING GOSPEL to preach unto them that the fly the Earth, and to every nation, and kindred, and tongue, and peaple —Rev. xiv. 6.

BY THE

REV. CLAUDIUS BUCHANAN D.D.

LATE VICE-PROVOST OF THE COLLEGE OF FORT-WILLIAM IN BENGAL.

NEW EDITION, CORRECTED.

LONDON:

WARD & CO. PATERNOSTER ROW.

LIVERPOOL:

EDWARD HOWELL, 6, CHURCH STREET, & PARK LANE.

1849.

CONTENTS.

CHRISTIAN RESEARCHES.

In his late discourses before the university of Cambridge, the author noticed incidentally some general circumstances of the darkness of paganism, and of the means which are now employed to diffuse the light of christianity in the east. This awakened a desire in some members of that learned body to know the particulars; for if there were a just expectation of success, and if the design were conducted in consonance with the principles and order of the church of England, it might be a proper subject for their countenance and co-operation. A more detailed account, therefore, will probably be read with interest. Many, doubtless, will rejoice to see the stream of divine knowledge, and civilization flowing to the utmost ends of the earth. And even those who have hitherto heard of the progress of christianity with little concern, may be induced to regard it with a humane solicitude.

In the college of Fort-William in Bengal, there was a department for translating the scriptures into the oriental languages; and, so early as 1805 (the fifth year of its institution) a commencement had been made in five languages. The first version of any of the gospels in the Persian and Hindostanee languages which were printed in India, issued from the press of the college of Fort-William. The Persian was superintended by Lieutenant-Colonel Colebrooke, and the Hindostanee by William Hunter, esq. The gospels were translated into the western Malay by Thomas Jarrett, esq. of the civil service; into the Orissa language by Pooroosh Ram, the Orissa

Pundit; and, into the Mahratta language by Vydyunath, the Mahratta Pundit, under the superintendence of Dr. William Carey.*

The college was founded on the 4th of May 1800. After it had flourished for almost seven years, during which period it produced nearly one hundred volumes in oriental literature,† the court of directors resolved on reducing its establishment within narrower limits on the 1st of January 1807. In consequence of this measure, the translations of the scriptures and some other literary works were suspended.

As this event had been long expected, the superintendents of the college, who were sensible of the importance of restoring sacred learning to the east, had begun, some time before, to consider of the means, by which that benefit might yet be secured. Much expense had already been incurred; many learned natives had come from remote regions to Calcutta, whose services could not be easily replaced; and who never could have been assembled, but by the influence of the supreme government, as exerted by the Marquis Wellesley. The court of directors were probably not fully aware of the importance of the works then carrying on, (although, indeed, their objection was not so much to the utility, as to the expense of the institution,) and it was believed that a time would come, when they would be happy to think that these works had not been permitted to fall to the ground. It was not, however, their causing the expense to cease which was the chief source of regret; but that the *unity* of the undertaking was now destroyed. The college of Fort-William had been identified with the church of England; and, under that character, had extended a liberal patronage to all learned men who could promote the translation of the scriptures. But now these translations being no longer subject to its revision, its responsibility would also cease.‡

* See "First four years of the College of Fort-William," p. 230. CADELL AND DAVIES.

† Ibid. 219.

‡ It will be gratifying to the public to learn that the college of Fort-William is now in a flourishing state, and has received the final sanction and patronage of the East India Company. It owes much to the cultivated mind and liberal spirit of Lord MINTO, the present governor-general of India; his Lordship had not been many months in that country, before he perceived its importance to the interests of the British Empire in the east; and his annual speeches at the public disputations, show that he thinks the college of Fort-William deserves

Under these circumstances the superintendents of the college resolved to encourage individuals to proceed with their versions by such means as they could command; and to trust to the contributions of the public, and to the future sanction of the government, for the perpetuity of the design. They purposed at the same time, not to confine the undertaking to Bengal alone, or to the territories of the company; but to extend it to every part of the east, where fit instruments for translation could be found. With this view, they aided the designs of the Baptist missionaries in Bengal, of the Lutheran missionaries in Coromandel belonging to "the Society for promoting Christian Knowledge," and of the other missionaries in the east connected with societies in England and Scotland: and also patronised those Roman catholic missionaries in the south of India whom they found qualified for conducting useful works. About the same period they exerted themselves in circulating proposals for the translation of the scriptures into the oriental languages, by the Baptist missionaries in Bengal among the English settlements in Asia, and in promoting subscriptions for that object by all the means in their power; and when it was proposed to the governor-general (Lord Minto, then just arrived) to suppress this mission, a memorial was addressed to the government in its behalf.

In order to obtain a distinct view of the state of chris-

as much of his attention and support as any department under his government. It will be yet more gratifying to many to hear that the college of Fort-William is likely to become once more a fountain of translation for the sacred scriptures. Dr. LEYDEN, professor of the Hindostanee language, has come forward (March 1810) with a proposal to superintend the translation of the scriptures into seven languages, hitherto little cultivated in India. This subject will be noticed hereafter.

It was expected that the East India college at Hertford would eventually supersede the college in Bengal; but it is obvious, that in order to give any efficiency to the purposes of a college at home, there must be also a college abroad. Little more than the elements of the oriental languages can be conveniently learnt in England. But this elementary labour at home is doubtless so much time saved in India. And thus far the institution at Hertford, independently of its other objects, is highly useful, in subserviency to the college of Fort-William. The two institutions combine the primary idea of Marquis Wellesley; and the expense is not less than that statesman had originally intended. There is this difference in the execution, that there are now two institutions instead of one. His Lordship proposed that the two institutions should be in India, combined in one; and his reasons were, that the organs of speech in youth are more flexible at an early age for learning a new language: and that the constitution of young persons assimilates more easily to a strange climate. There are various advantages however in having the elementary institution at home which may counterbalance these reasons; and if it continue to be conducted with the same spirit and effect which have hitherto distinguished it, I think that the present plan is preferable.

tianity and of superstition in Asia, the superintendents of the college had, before this period, entered into correspondence with intelligent persons in different countries; and, from every quarter, (even from the confines of China) they received encouragement to proceed. But, as contradictory accounts were given by different writers concerning the real state of the numerous tribes in India, both of christians and natives, the author conceived the design of devoting the last year or two of his residence in the east, to purposes of local examination and inquiry. With this view, he travelled through the peninsula of India by land, from Calcutta to Cape Comorin, a continent extending through fourteen degrees of latitude, and visited Ceylon thrice. And he soon discovered that a person may reside all his life in Bengal, and yet know almost as little of other countries in India, for instance, of Travancore, Ceylon, Goa, or Madura, of their manners, customs, habits and religion, as if he had never left England.* The principal objects of this tour, were to investigate the state of superstition at the most celebrated temples of the Hindoos; to examine the churches and libraries of the Romish, Syrian, and protestant christians; to ascertain the present state and recent history of the eastern Jews; and to discover what persons might be fit instruments for the promotion of learning in their respective countries, and for maintaining a future correspondence on the subject of disseminating the scriptures in India. In pursuance of these objects the author visited Cuttack, Ganjam, Visagapatam, Samulcotta, Rajamundry, Ellore, Ongole, Nellore, Madras, Mailapoor, Pondicherry, Cudalore, Tranquebar, Tanjore, Tritchinopoly, Aughoor, Madura, Palamcotta, Ramnad, Jaffna-patam, Columbo, Manaar, Tutecorin, Augengo, Quilon, Cochin, Cranganor, Verapoli, Calicut, Tellicherry, Goa, and other places between Cape Comorin and Bombay; the interior of Travancore and the interior of Malabar; also seven principal temples of the Hindoos, viz. Seemachalum in the Telinga country, Chillumbrum, Seringham, Madura, Ramisseram, Elephanta, and Juggernaut.

* Of the books published in Britain on the discussion relating to missions and the state of India, the most sensible and authentic are, in general, those written by learned men of the universities who have never been in the east.

After this tour, the author returned to Calcutta, where he remained about three quarters of a year longer, and then visited the Jews and the Syrian christians in Malabar and Travancore a second time before his return to England.

Those nations or communities for whom translations of the scriptures have been commenced under the patronage or direction already alluded to, are the following: the Chinese, the Hindoos, the Cingalese or Ceylonese, the Malays, the Syrian christians, the Romish christians, the Persians, the Arabians, and the Jews. Of these it is proposed to give some account in their order.

THE CHINESE.

In the discussions concerning the promulgation of christianity, some writers have confined their views entirely to India, merely, it is supposed, because India is connected, by political relation, with Great Britain. India however contains but a small part of the nations which seek the revelation of God. The Malayan Archipelago includes more territory and a larger population than the continent of India. China is a more extensive field than either; and is, in some respects, far more important. The Romish church has maintained a long and ineffectual contest with that empire; because it would never give the people, "the good and perfect gift," the Bible. It further degraded the doctrine of the cross by blending it with Pagan rites.

The means of obtaining a version of the scriptures in the Chinese language, occupied the minds of the superintendents of the college of Fort-William, at an early period. It appeared an object of the utmost importance to procure an erudite professor who should undertake such a work; for, if but a single copy of the scriptures could be introduced into China, they might be transcribed in almost every part of that immense empire. Another object in view was to introduce some knowledge of the Chinese language among ourselves; for although the Chinese forts on the Thibet frontier overlook the company's territories in Bengal, there was not a person, it was said, in the company's service in India, who could read a common Chinese letter.

After a long inquiry they succeeded in procuring Mr. Joannes Lassar, an Armenian christian, a native of China and a proficient in the Chinese language, who had been employed by the Portuguese at Macao, in conducting their official correspondence with the court of Pekin. He was willing to relinquish his commercial pursuits and to attach himself to the college, for a salary of £450 a year. But as the order for reducing the establishment of the college was daily expected, this salary could not be given him. The object however was so important, and Mr. Lassar appeared to be so well qualified to execute it, that they thought fit to retain him at the above stipend in a private character. He entered immediately on the translation of the scriptures into the Chinese language, and this work he has continued to carry on to the present time. But, as his services might be made otherwise useful, they resolved to establish a class of youths under his tuition; and as they could not obtain the young civil servants of the company for this purpose, they proposed to the Baptist missionaries that Mr. Lassar should reside at Serampore, which is near Calcutta, on the following condition: that one of their elder missionaries, and three at least of their youths, should immediately engage in the study of the Chinese language. Dr. Carey declined the offer, but Mr. Marshman accepted it, and was joined by two sons of his own, and a son of Dr. Carey; and they have prosecuted their studies with unremitted attention for about five years.

In the year 1807, a copy of the gospel of St. Matthew in the Chinese language, translated by Mr. Lassar, and beautifully written by himself, was transmitted to his Grace the Archbishop of Canterbury for the Lambeth library.—Since that period a considerable portion of the New Testament has been printed off from blocks, after the Chinese manner.

The proficiency of the Chinese pupils has far surpassed the most sanguine hopes which were previously entertained, and has been already publicly noticed. His excellency Lord Minto, governor-general of India, in his first annual speech to the college of Fort-William, has recorded the following testimony to their progress in the language, and to the importance of their attainments.

"If I have not passed beyond the legitimate bounds of this discourse, in ranging to the extremity of those countries, and to the furthest island of that vast Archipelago in which the *Malay* language prevails, I shall scarcely seem to transgress them, by the short and easy transition thence to the language of CHINA. I am, in truth, strongly inclined, whether regularly or not, to deal one encouraging word to the meritorious, and, I hope, not unsuccessful effort, making, I may say, at the door of our college, though not admitted to its portico, to force that hitherto impregnable fortress, the Chinese language. Three young men, I ought indeed to say, boys, have not only acquired a ready use of the Chinese language, for the purpose of oral communication (which I understand is neither difficult nor rare amongst Europeans connected with China) but they have achieved, in a degree worthy of admiration, that which has been deemed scarcely within the reach of European faculties or industry; I mean a very extensive and correct acquaintance with the written language of China. I will not detail the particulars of the examination which took place on the 10th of this month (February 1808) at Serampore, in the Chinese language, the report of which I have read, however, with great interest, and recommended to the liberal notice of those whom I have the honour to address. It is enough for my present purpose to say that these young pupils read Chinese books and translate them; and they write compositions of their own in the Chinese language and character. A Chinese PRESS too is established, and in actual use. In a word, if the founders and supporters of this little college have not yet dispelled, they have at least sent and admitted a dawn of day through that thick impenetrable cloud; they have passed that *Oceanum dissociabilem,* which for so many ages has insulated that vast empire from the rest of mankind."

"I must not omit to commend the zealous and persevering labours of Mr. LASSAR, and of those learned and pious persons associated with him, who have accomplished, for the future benefit, we may hope, of that immense and populous region, CHINESE VERSIONS in the Chinese character, of the Gospels of Matthew, Mark, and Luke, throwing open that precious mine, with all its religious and moral treasure to the largest associated population in the world."*

When this Chinese class was first established, it was directed that there should be regular public examinations and disputations, as at the college of Fort-William. The examination in September 1808, (a few months after the above speech of Lord Minto was pronounced) was held in the presence of J. H. Harington, esq. vice-president of the Asiatic society, Dr. John Leyden, and other oriental scholars; when the three youths, mentioned above, maintained a disputation in the Chinese language. On this occasion, the respondent defended the following position: "To commit to memory the Chinese classics is the best mode of acquiring the Chinese language."

One most valuable effect of these measures is a work just published by Mr. Joshua Marshman, the elder pupil of Mr. Lassar. It is the first volume of "the works of Confucius containing the original text, with a translation; to which is prefixed, a dissertation on the Chinese language, pp. 877, 4to;" to be followed by four volumes more. This translation will be received with gratitude by the learned, and will be considered as a singular monument of the indefatigable labour of an English missionary in the acquisition of a new language.

While treating of the cultivation of the Chinese language, it will be proper to notice the endeavours of the London missionary society in the same department. While Mr. Lassar and Mr. Marshman are translating the scriptures at Calcutta, Mr. Morrison is prosecuting a similar work at Canton in China, with the aid of able native scholars. It is stated in the report of their society, that the principal difficulties have been surmounted, and that the period of his acquiring a complete knowledge of the language is by no means so distant as what he once expected. "It has proved of great advantage to him that he copied and carried out with him the Chinese translation of the gospels preserved in the British museum, which he now finds from his own increasing acquaintance with the language, and the opinion of the Chinese assistants, to be exceedingly valuable, and

* See college report for 1808.

which must, from the excellency of the style, have been produced by Chinese natives." He adds, that the manuscript of the New Testament is fit to be printed; and that he proposes to publish also a Dictionary and a Grammar of the language, the last of which is already "prepared for the press."* The expense to the London missionary society for the current year, in the Chinese department alone, is stated to be £500.

The foregoing notices of the progress of Chinese literature will, I doubt not, be acceptable to many; for the cultivation of the Chinese language, considered merely in a political point of view, must prove of the utmost advantage to this country, in her further transactions with that ancient and ingenious, but jealous, incommunicative and partially civilized nation.

THE HINDOOS.

It is admitted by all writers that the civilization of the Hindoos will be promoted by intercourse with the English. But this only applies to that small portion of the natives, who live in the vicinity of Europeans, and mix with them. As for the bulk of the population, they scarcely ever see an Englishman. It becomes then of importance "to ascertain what have been the actual effects of christianity in those interior provinces of Hindostan, where it has been introduced by the christian missionaries;" and to compare them with such of their countrymen as remain in their pristine idolatry. It was a chief object of the author's tour through India, to mark the relative influence of paganism and christianity. In order then that the English nation may be able to form a judgment on this subject, he will proceed to give some account of the Hindoos of *Juggernaut*, and of the native christians in *Tanjore*. The Hindoos of Juggernaut have as yet had no advantages of christian instruction: and continue to worship the idol called Juggernaut. The native christians of Tanjore, until the light of revelation visited them, worshipped an idol also, called the great black bull of Tanjore. And, as in this brief work the author proposes to state merely what

* Report of London missionary society for 1810, p. 22.

he himself has seen, with little comment or observation, it will suffice to give a few extracts from the journal of his tour through these provinces.

EXTRACTS from the AUTHOR'S JOURNAL in his tour to the temple of Juggernaut in Orissa, in the year 1806.

"*Buddruck in Orissa, May 30th,* 1806.

"We know that we are approaching Juggernaut (and yet we are more than fifty miles from it) by the human bones which we have seen for some days strewed by the way. At this place we have been joined by several large bodies of pilgrims, perhaps 2,000 in number, who have come from various parts of northern India; some of them, with whom I have conversed, say that they have been two months on their march, travelling slowly in the hottest season of the year, with their wives and children. Some old persons are among them who wish to die at Juggernaut. Numbers of pilgrims die on the road; and their bodies generally remain unburied. On a plain by the river, near the pilgrims' caravansera at this place, there are more than a hundred sculls. The dogs, jackals, and vultures, seem to live here on human prey. The vultures exhibit a shocking *tameness*. The obscene animals will not leave the body sometimes till we come close to them. This Buddruck is a horrid place. Wherever I turn my eyes, I meet death in some shape or other. Surely Juggernaut cannot be worse than Buddruck."

"*In sight of Juggernaut, 12th June.*

"Many thousands of pilgrims have accompanied us for some days past, they cover the road before and behind as far as the eye can reach. At nine o'clock this morning, the temple of Juggernaut appeared in view at a great distance; when the multitude first saw it, they gave a shout, and fell to the ground and worshipped. I have heard nothing to-day but shouts and acclamations by the successive bodies of pilgrims. From the place where I now stand I have a view of a host of people like an army, encamped at the outer gate of the town of

Juggernaut; where a guard of soldiers is posted to prevent their entering the town, until they have paid the pilgrim's tax.—I passed a devotee to-day who laid himself down at every step, measuring the road to Juggernaut, by the *length of his body*, as a penance of merit to please the god."

"*Outer gate of Juggernaut, 12th June.*

"A disaster has just occurred.—As I approached the gate, the pilgrims crowded from all quarters around me, and shouted, as they usually did when I passed them on the road, an expression of welcome and respect; I was a little alarmed at their number, and looked round for my guard. A guard of soldiers had accompanied me from Cuttack, the last military station; but they were now about a quarter of a mile behind, with my servants and the baggage. The pilgrims cried out that they were entitled to some indulgence, that they were poor, that they could not pay the tax; but I was not aware of their design. At this moment, when I was within a few yards of the gate, an old Sanyassee (or holy man) who had travelled some days by the side of my horse, came up and said, 'Sir, you are in danger; the people are going to rush through the gate when it is opened for you.' I immediately dismounted, and endeavoured to escape to one side; but it was too late. The mob was now in motion, and with a tumultuous shout pressed violently towards the gate; the guard within seeing my danger opened it, and the multitude rushing through, carried me forward in the torrent a considerable space; so that I was literally borne into Juggernaut by the Hindoos themselves. A distressing scene followed. As the number and strength of the mob increased, the narrow way was choked up by the mass of people; and I apprehended that many of them would have been suffocated, or bruised to death. My horse was yet among them, but suddenly one of the side posts of the gate, which was of wood, gave way and fell to the ground; and perhaps this circumstance alone prevented the loss of lives. Notice of the event was immediately communicated to Mr. Hunter, the superintendent of the temple, who repaired to the spot, and sent an additional guard to the inner gate, lest the people should force that also; for there is an outer and an inner gate to the town of Juggernaut; but both of them are slightly constructed. Mr. Hunter told me that similar accidents sometimes occur, and that many have been crushed to death by the pressure of the mob. He added, that sometimes a body of pilgrims (consisting chiefly of women and children and old men) trusting to the physical weight of their mass, will make, what he called, a *charge* on the armed guards, and overwhelm them; the guards not being willing in such circumstances, to oppose their bayonets."

"*Juggernaut, 14th June.*

"I have seen Juggernaut; the scene at Buddruck is but the vestibule to Juggernaut; no record of ancient or modern history can give, I think, an adequate idea of this valley of death; it may be truly compared with the 'valley of Hinnom.' The idol called Juggernaut, has been considered as the Moloch of the present age; and he is justly so named, for the sacrifices offered up to him by self-devotement, are not less criminal, perhaps not less numerous, than those recorded of the Moloch of Canaan. Two other idols accompany Juggernaut, namely, Boloram and Shubudra, his brother and sister; for there are *three* deities worshipped here. They receive equal adoration and sit on thrones of nearly equal height."

"This morning I viewed the temple; a stupendous fabric, and truly commensurate with the extensive sway of 'the horrid king.' As other temples are usually adorned with figures emblematical of their religion; so Juggernaut has representations (numerous and various) of that vice, which constitutes the essence of *his* worship. The walls and gates are covered with indecent emblems, in massive and durable sculpture.—I have also visited the sand plains by the sea, in some places whitened with the bones of the pilgrims; and another place a little way out of the town, called by the English, the Golgotha, where the dead bodies are usually cast forth; and where dogs and vultures are ever seen.*

* The vultures generally find out the prey first: and begin with the intestines; for the flesh of the body is too firm for their beaks immediately after

"The grand Hindoo festival of the Rutt Jattra, takes place on the 18th inst. when the idol is to be brought forth to the people. I reside during my stay here at the house of James Hunter, esq. the company's collector of the tax on pilgrims, and superintendant of the temple, formerly a student in the college of Fort-William; by whom I am hospitably entertained, and also by Captain Patten, and Lieut. Woodcock, commanding the military force. Mr. Hunter distinguished himself at the college by his proficiency in the Oriental language; he is a gentleman of polished manners, and of classical taste. The agreeable society of these gentlemen is very refreshing to my spirits in the midst of the present scenes; I was surprised to see how little they seemed to be moved by the scenes of Juggernaut. They said they were now so accustomed to them, they thought little of them, they had almost forgot their first impressions; their houses are on the sea shore, about a mile or more from the temple, they cannot live nearer, on account of the offensive effluvia of the town, for independently of the enormity of the superstition, there are other circumstances which render Juggernaut noisome in an extreme degree; the senses are assailed by the squalid and ghastly appearance of the famished pilgrims; many of whom die in the streets of want or of disease; while the devotees with clotted hair and painted flesh, are seen practising their various austerities, and modes of self-torture. Persons of both sexes, with little regard to concealment, sit down on the sands close to the town, in public view; and the SACRED BULLS walk about among them and eat the *ordure**.

"The vicinity of Juggernaut to the sea probably prevents the contagion, which otherwise would be produced by the putrefactions of the place.—There is scarcely any verdure to refresh the sight near Juggernaut; the temple and town being nearly encompassed by the hills of

death. But the dogs soon receive notice of the circumstance, generally from seeing the hurries or corpse-carriers returning from the place. On the approach of the dogs, the vultures retire a few yards, and wait till the body be sufficiently torn for easy deglutition. The vultures and dogs often feed together; and sometimes begin their attack before the pilgrim be quite dead. There are four animals which are sometimes seen about a carcase, the dog, the jackal, the vulture, and the burgeela, or adjutant, called by Pennant, the gigantic crane.

* This singular fact was pointed out to me by the gentlemen here. There is no vegetation for the sacred bulls on these sand plains, they are fed generally with vegetables from the hands of the pilgrims.

sand, which have been cast up in the lapse of ages, by the surge of the ocean. All is barren and desolate to the eye; and in the ear there is the never intermitting sound of the roaring sea."

"*Juggernaut*, 18*th of June*.

"I have returned home from witnessing a scene which I shall never forget. At twelve o'clock of this day, being the great day of the feast, the Moloch of Hindoostan was brought out of his temple amidst the acclamations of hundreds of thousands of his worshippers; when the idol was placed on his throne, a shout was raised, by the multitude, such as I had never heard before; it continued equable for a few minutes, and then gradually died away. After a short interval of silence, a murmur was heard at a distance; all eyes were turned towards the place, and behold, a *grove* advancing! a body of men, having green branches, or palms in their hands, approached with great celerity. The people opened a way for them; and when they had come up to the throne, they fell down before him that sat thereon, and worshipped. And the multitude again sent forth a voice 'like the sound of a great thunder'—but the voices I now heard, were not those of melody or of joyful acclamation; for there is no harmony in the praise of Moloch's worshippers. Their number indeed brought to my mind the countless multitude of the Revelations; but their voices gave no tuneful Hosannah or Hallelujah; but rather a yell of approbation, united with a kind of *hissing* applause.*—I was at a loss how to account for this latter noise, until I was directed to notice the women, who emitted a sound like that of *whistling*, with the lips circular, and the tongue vibrating, as if a serpent would speak by their organs, uttering human sounds.

"The throne of the idol was placed on a stupendous car or tower, about sixty feet in height, resting on wheels which indented the ground deeply, as they turned slowly under the ponderous machine. Attached to it were six cables, of the size and length of a ship's cable, by which

* See Milton's Pandemonium, Book X.

the people drew it along. Upon the tower were the priests and satellites of the idol, surrounding his throne. The idol is a block of wood, having a frightful visage painted black, with a distended mouth of a bloody colour, his arms are of gold, and he is dressed in gorgeous apparel. The other two idols are of a white and yellow colour.—Five elephants preceded the three towers, bearing towering flags, dressed in crimson caparisons, and having bells hanging to their caparisons, which sounded musically as they moved.

"I went on in the procession, close by the tower of Moloch; which, as it was drawn with difficulty, grated on its many wheels harsh thunder.* After a few minutes it stopped; and now the worship of the God began.—A high priest mounted the car in front of the idol, and pronounced his obscene stanzas in the ears of the people; who responded at intervals in the same strain. 'These songs,' said he, 'are the delight of the God: his car can only move when he is pleased with the 'song.'—The car moved on a little way and then stopped.—A boy of about twelve years was then brought fourth to attempt something yet more lascivious, if peradventure the God would move; the 'child perfected the praise' of his idol with such ardent expression and gesture, that the god was pleased, and the multitude emitting a sensual yell of delight, urged the car along.—After a few minutes it stopped again. An aged minister of the idol then stood up, and with a long rod in his hand, which he moved with indecent action, completed the variety of this disgusting exhibition.—I felt a consciousness of doing wrong in witnessing it. I was also somewhat appalled at the magnitude and horror of the spectacle. I felt like a guilty person, on whom all eyes were fixed, and I was about to withdraw; but a scene

* Two of the military gentlemen had mounted my elephant that they might witness the spectacle, and had brought him close to the tower; but the moment it began to move, the animal, alarmed at the unusual noise, took fright and ran off through the crowd till he was stopped by a wall. The natural fear of the elephant, lest he should injure human life, was remarkably exemplified on this occasion. Though the crowd was very closely set, he endeavoured, in the midst of his own terror, to throw the people off on both sides with his feet, and it was found that he had only trod upon one person. It was with great concern I afterwards learnt that this was a poor woman, and that the fleshy part of her leg had been torn off. There being no medical person here, Lieut. Woodcock with great humanity endeavoured to dress the wound and attended her daily; and Mr. Hunter ordered her to be supplied with every thing that might conduce to her recovery.

of a different kind was now to be presented. The characteristics of Moloch's worship are obscenity and blood. We have seen the former—now comes the blood!

"After the tower had proceeded some way, a pilgrim announced that he was ready to offer himself a sacrifice to the idol. He laid himself down in the road before the tower as it was moving along, lying on his face, with his arms stretched forwards; the multitude passed round him, leaving the space clear, and he was crushed to death by the wheels of the tower. A shout of joy was raised to the God; he is said to *smile* when the libation of the blood is made; the people threw cowries, or small money, on the body of the victim, in approbation of the deed. He was left to view a considerable time, and was then carried by the *Hurries* to the Golgotha, where I have just been viewing his remains. How much I wished that the proprietors of India stock could have attended the wheels of Juggernaut, and seen this peculiar source of their revenue."

"*Juggernaut*, 20*th June*.

> "Moloch, horrid king, besmeared with blood
> Of human sacrifice, and parents' tears." MILTON.

"——The horrid solemnities still continue. Yesterday a woman devoted herself to the idol. She laid herself down on the road in an oblique direction, so that the wheel did not kill her instantaneously, as is generally the case; but she died in a few hours. This morning as I passed the Place of Skulls, nothing remained of her but her bones.

"And this, thought I, is the worship of the Brahmins of Hindoostan! and their worship in its sublimest degree! What then shall we think of their private manners, and their moral principles! for it is equally true of India as of Europe, if you would know the state of the people, look at the state of the temple.

"I was surprised to see the Brahmins with their heads uncovered in the open plain falling down in the midst of the *Sooders* before 'the horrid shape,' and mingling so complacently with 'that polluted cast.' But this proved what I had before heard, that so great a

God is this, that the dignity of high cast disappears before him. This great king recognises no distinction of rank among his subjects; all men are equal in his presence."

"*Juggernaut*, 21*st June*.

"The idolatrous processions continue for some days longer, but my spirits are so exhausted by the constant view of these enormities, that I mean to hasten away from this place sooner than I at first intended.—I beheld another distressing scene this morning at the Place of Skulls;—a poor woman lying dead, or nearly dead, and her two children by her, looking at the dogs and vultures which were near. The people passed by without noticing the children. I asked them where was their home. They said, 'they had no home but where their mother was.'—O, there is no pity at Juggernaut! no mercy, no tenderness of heart in Moloch's kingdom! Those who support *his* kingdom, err, I trust, from ignorance. 'They know not what they do.'"

"As to the number of worshippers assembled here at this time, no accurate calculation can be made. The natives themselves, when speaking of the numbers at particular festivals, usually say that a lack of people (100,000) would not be missed. I asked a Brahmin how many he supposed were present at the most numerous festival he had ever witnessed. 'How can I tell,' said he, 'how many grains there are in a handful of sand?'

"The languages spoken here are various, as there are Hindoos from every country in India; but the two chief languages in use by those who are resident, are the Orissa and the Telinga. The border of the Telinga country is only a few miles distant from the tower of Juggernaut."

"*Chilka Lake*, 24*th June*.

"—— I felt my mind relieved and happy when I had passed beyond the confines of Juggernaut. I certainly was not prepared for the scene; but no one can know what it is who has not seen it.—From an eminence* on the pleasant banks of the Chilka Lake (where no human bones are seen), I had a view of the lofty tower of Juggernaut far remote; and while I viewed it, its abominations came to mind. It was on the morning of the sabbath; ruminating long on the wide and extended empire of Moloch in the heathen world, I cherished in my thoughts the design of some 'Christian Institution,' which being fostered by Britain, my christian country, might gradually undermine this baleful idolatry, and put out the memory of it for ever."

Annual expenses of the Idol JUGGERNAUT, *presented to the English Government.*

[Extracted from the Official Accounts.]

		Rupees	£sterling
1.	Expenses attending the table of the idol	36,115 or	4,514
2.	Ditto of his dress or wearing apparel	2,712	339
3.	Ditto of the wages of his servants	10,057	1,259
4.	Ditto of contingent expenses at the different seasons of pilgrimage	10,989	1,373
5.	Ditto of his elephants and horses.	3,030	378
6.	Ditto of his rutt or annual state carriage	6,713	839
	Rupees	69,616	£8,702

"In item third, 'wages of his servants,' are included the wages of the *courtesans*, who are kept for the service of the temple.

"Item sixth.—What is here called in the official account 'the state carriage,' is the same as the car or tower. Mr. Hunter informed me that the three 'state carriages' were decorated this year (in June 1806) with upwards of £200 sterling worth of English *broad cloth* and *baize*.

* Manickpatam.

"Of the rites celebrated in the interior of Juggernaut, called the *daily service*, I can say nothing of my own knowledge, not having been within the Temple." *

JUGGERNAUT IN BENGAL.

Lest it should be supposed that the rites of Juggernaut are confined to the temple in Orissa, or that the Hindoos there practice a more criminal superstition than they do in other places, it may be proper to notice the effects of the same idolatry in Bengal. The English nation will not expect to hear that the blood of Juggernaut is known at Calcutta; but, alas, it is shed at the very doors of the English, almost under the eye of the supreme government. Moloch has many a tower in the province of Bengal; that fair and fertile province which has been called "The Garden of Nations." Close to Ishera, a beautiful villa on the river's side, about eight miles from Calcutta, once the residence of Governor Hastings, and within view of the present Govenor-General's country-house, there is a temple of this idol which is often stained with human blood. At the festival of the Rutt Jattra in May 1807, the author visited it, on his return from the South of India, having heard that its rites were similar to those of Juggernaut.

* The temple of Juggernaut is under the immediate control of the English Government, who levy a tax on pilgrims as a source of revenue. See "A regulation (by the Bengal Government) for levying a tax from pilgrims resorting to the temple of Juggernaut, and for the superintendance and management of the temple. Passed April 3, 1806."

The province of Orissa first became subject to the British empire under the administration of the Marquis Wellesley, who permitted the pilgrims at first to visit Juggernaut without paying tribute. It was proposed to his Lordship, soon after, to pass the above regulation for the management of the temple, and levying the tax; but he did not approve of it, and actually left the Government without giving his sanction to the opprobrious law. When the measure was discussed by the succeeding Government, it was resisted by George Udny, esq. one of the members of the Supreme Council, who recorded his solemn dissent on the proceedings of Government, for transmission to England. The other members considered Juggernaut to be a legitimate source of revenue, on the principle, I believe, that money from other temples in Hindoostan had long been brought into the treasury. It is just that I should state that these gentlemen (though their opinion on this subject will differ so much from that of their countrymen at home) are men of the most honourable principles and of unimpeached integrity. Nor would any one of them, I believe, (for I have the honour to know them), do any thing which he thought injurious to the honour or religion of his country. But the truth is this, that those persons who go to India in early youth, and witness the Hindoo customs all their life, seeing little at the same time of the christian religion to counteract the effect, are disposed to view them with complacency, and are sometimes in danger of at length considering them even as proper or necessary.

"*Juggernaut's Temple, near Ishera, on the Ganges:*
"*Rutt Jattra, May*, 1807.

"The tower here is drawn along, like that at Juggernaut, by cables. The number of worshippers at this festival is computed to be about a hundred thousand. The tower is covered with indecent emblems, which were freshly painted for the occasion, and were the objects of sensual gaze by *both* sexes. One of the victims of this year was a well made young man, of healthy appearance and comely aspect. He had a garland of flowers round his neck, and his long black hair was dishevelled. He danced for awhile before the idol, singing in an enthusiastic strain, and then rushing suddenly to the wheels, he shed his blood under the tower of obscenity. I was not at the spot at the time, my attention having been engaged by a more pleasing scene.

"On the other side, on a rising ground by the side of a tank, stood the christian missionaries, and around them a crowd of people listening to their preaching. The town of Serampore, where the Protestant missionaries reside, is only about a mile and a half from this temple of Juggernaut. As I passed through the multitude, I met several persons having the printed papers of the missionaries in their hands. Some of them were reading them very gravely; others were laughing with each other at the contents, and saying, 'What do these words mean?'"

"I sat down on an elevated spot to contemplate this scene,—the tower of blood and impurity on the one hand, and the christian preachers on the other. I thought on the commandment of our Saviour, 'Go ye, teach all nations.' I said to myself, 'How great and glorious a ministry are these humble persons now exercising in the presence of God!' How is it applauded by the holy angels, who 'have joy in heaven over one sinner that repenteth;' and how far does it transcend the work of the warrior or statesman, in charity, utility, and lasting fame! And I could not help wishing that the representatives of the church of Christ in my own country had been present to witness this scene, that they might have seen how practicable it is to offer christian instruction to our Hindoo subjects."

IMMOLATION OF FEMALES.

Before the author proceeds to shew the happy effects of christianity in those provinces of India where it has been introduced, it may be proper to notice in this place that other sanguinary rite of the Hindoo superstition, the FEMALE SACRIFICE. The report of the number of women burned within the period of six months near Calcutta, will give the reader some idea of the multitude who perish annually in India.

"Report of the number of women who were burned alive on the funeral pile of their husbands, within thirty miles round Calcutta, from the beginning of Bysakh (15th April) to the end of Aswin (15th October) 1804."

	Women burned alive.
From Gurria to Barrypore; at eleven different places*	18
From Tolly's Nullah mouth to Gurria; at seventeen different places	36
From Barrypore to Buhipore; at seven places	11
From Seebpore to Balleea; at five places	10
From Balee to Bydyabattee; at three places	3
From Bydyabattee to Bassbareea; at five places	10
From Calcutta to Burahnugur (or Barnagore); at four places . .	6
From Burahnugur to Chanok (or Barrackpore); at six places . .	13
From Channok to Kachrapara; at four places	8
Total of women burned alive in six months, near Calcutta .	115

"The above report was made by persons of the Hindoo cast, deputed for that purpose, under the superintendance of the Professor of the Sanscrit and Bengalee languages in the College of Fort-William. They were ten in number, and were stationed at different places during the whole period of six months. They gave in their account monthly, specifying the particulars of each immolation, so that every individual instance was subject to investigation immediately after its occurrence.

"By an account taken in 1803, the number of women sacrificed during that year, within thirty miles round Calcutta, was two hundred and seventy-five.

"In the foregoing report of six months in 1804, it will be perceived that no account was taken of burnings

* See the names of the places and other particulars in 'Memoir of the Expediency of an Ecclesiastical Establisment in British India,' p. 102.

in a district to the west of Calcutta, nor further than twenty miles in some other directions; so that the whole number of burnings within thirty miles round Calcutta must have been considerably greater than is here stated."

The following account will give the reader some idea of the flagitious circumstances which sometimes attend these sacrifices.

SACRIFICE OF THE KOOLIN BRAHMIN'S THREE WIVES.

"*Calcutta, 30th Sept.* 1807.

"A horrid tragedy was acted, on the 12th instant, near Barnagore (a place about three miles above Calcutta). A Koolin Brahmin of Cammar-hattie, by name Kristo Deb Mookerjee, died at the advanced age of ninety-two. He had twelve wives:* and three of them were burned alive with his dead body. Of these three, one was a venerable lady, having white locks, who had been long known in the neighbourhood. Not being able to walk, she was carried in a palanquin to the place of burning; and was then placed by the Brahmins on the funeral pile. The two other ladies were younger; one of them of a very pleasing and interesting countenance. The old lady was placed on one side of the dead husband, and the two other wives laid themselves down on the other side; and then an old Brahmin, the eldest son of the deceased, applied his torch to the pile, with unaverted face. The pile suddenly blazed, for it was covered with combustibles; and this human sacrifice was completed amidst the din of drums and symbals, and the shouts of Brahmins.—A person present observed, 'Surely if Lord Minto were here, who is just come from

* The Koolin Brahmin is the purest of all Brahmins, and is privileged to marry as many wives as he pleases. The Hindoo families account it an honour to unite their daughters with a Koolin Brahmin. "The Ghantucks or Registrars of the Koolin cast state that Rajeb Bonnerjee, now of Calcutta, has forty wives; and that Raj-chunder Bonnerjee, also of Calcutta, has forty-two wives, and intends to marry more: that Ramraja Bonnerjee, of Bicrampore, aged thirty years, and Pooran Bonnerjee, Rijkissore Chutterjee, and Roopram Mookerjee, have each upwards of forty wives, and intend to marry more; that Birjoo Mookerjee, of Bicrampore, who died about five years ago, had ninety wives." This account was authenticated at Calcutta in the year 1804. See further particulars in the "Memoir" before quoted, p. 111.

England, and is not used to see women burned alive, he would have saved these three ladies.' The Mahomedan Governors saved whom they pleased, and suffered no deluded female to commit suicide, without previous investigation of the circumstances, and official permission.

"In a discussion which this event has produced in Calcutta, the following question has been asked, WHO WAS GUILTY OF THE BLOOD OF THE OLD LADY? for it was manifest that she could not destroy herself. She *was carried* to be burned. It was also alleged that the Brahmin who fired the pile was not guilty, because he was never informed by the English Government that there was any immorality in the action; on the contrary, he might argue that the English, witnessing this scene daily, as they do, without remonstrance, acquiesced in its propriety. The Government in India was exculpated, on the ground that the Government at home never sent any instructions on the subject; and the Court of Directors were exculpated, because they were the agents of others. It remained that the proprietors of India stock, who originate and sanction all proceedings of the Court of Directors, were remotely accessary to the deed."

The best vindication of the great body of the proprietors is this, that some of them never heard of the female sacrifice at all; and that few of them are acquainted with the full extent and frequency of the crime.—Besides, in the above discussion, it was taken for granted that the Court of Directors have done nothing towards the suppression of this enormity; and that the Court of proprietors have looked on, without concern, at this omission of duty. But this, perhaps, may not be the case. The question then remains to be asked,—Have the Court of Directors at any time sent instructions to their Government in India, to report on the means by which the frequency of the female sacrifice might be diminished, and the practice itself eventually abolished? *Or have the Proprietors of India stock at any time instructed the Court of Directors to attend to a point of so much consequence to the character of the Company, and the honour of the nation?*

That the abolition is practicable has been demonstrated; and that too by the most rational and lenient measures; and these means have been pointed out by the Brahmins themselves.*

Had Marquis Wellesley remained in India, and been permitted to complete his salutary plans for the improvement of that distant empire, (for he did not finish one half of the civil and political regulations which he had in view, and had actually commenced) the female sacrifice would probably have been by this time nearly abolished.† The humanity and intrepid spirit of that nobleman abolished a yet more criminal practice which was considered by the Hindoos as a religious rite, and consecrated by custom, I mean the SACRIFICE of CHILDREN. His Lordship had been informed that it had been a custom of the Hindoos to sacrifice children in consequence of vows, by drowning them, or exposing them to sharks and crocodiles; and that twenty-three persons had perished at Saugor in one month (January 1801,) many of whom were sacrificed in this manner. He immediately instituted an inquiry into the principle of this ancient atrocity, heard what natives and Europeans had to say on the subject; and then passed a law, "declaring the practice to be murder, punishable by death."—The law is entitled "A regulation for preventing the sacrifice of children at Saugor and other places; passed by the Governor-General in Council on the 20th of August, 1802."—The purpose of this regulation was completely effected; not a murmur was heard on the subject; nor has any attempt of the kind come to our knowledge since. It is impossible to calculate the number of human lives that have been saved, during the last eight years, by this humane law of Marquis Wellesley.—Now it is well known that it is as easy to prevent the sacrifice of women as the sacrifice of children. Has this fact ever been denied by any one who is competent to offer a judgment on the subject? Until the supreme Government in Bengal shall declare that it is utterly impracticable to lessen the frequency of the immolation of females by any means, THE AUTHOR WILL NOT CEASE TO CALL THE ATTENTION OF THE ENGLISH NATION TO THIS SUBJECT.

* See them detailed in Memoir, p. 49.

† Ibid. p. 47.

TANJORE.

THE letters of KING GEORGE the FIRST to the Missionaries in India, will form a proper introduction to the account which it is now intended to give of the christian Hindoos of Tanjore. The first Protestant mission in India was founded by Bartholomew Ziegenbalg, a man of erudition and piety, educated at the university of Halle in Germany. He was ordained by the learned Burmannus, bishop of Zealand in his twenty-third year, and sailed for India in 1705. In the second year of his ministry he founded a christian church among the Hindoos, which has been extending its limits to the present time. In 1714, he returned to Europe for a short time, and on that occasion was honoured with an audience by His Majesty George the First, who took much interest in the success of the mission. He was also patronized by "the Society for promoting Christian Knowledge," which was superintended by men of distinguished learning and piety. The king and the society encouraged the Oriental missionary to proceed in his translation of the Scriptures into the *Tamul* tongue, which they designated "the grand work." This was indeed THE GRAND WORK; for wherever the scriptures are translated into the vernacular tongue, and are open and common to all, inviting inquiry and causing discussion, they cannot remain "a dead letter." When the scriptures speak to a heathen in his own tongue, his conscience responds, "this is the word of God." How little is the importance of a version of the Bible in a new language understood by some! The man who produces a translation of the Bible into a new language (like Wickliff, and Luther, and Ziegenbalg, and Carey) is a greater benefactor to mankind than the prince who founds an empire. For the "incorruptible seed of the word of God" can never die. After ages have revolved, it is still producing new accessions to truth and human happiness.

In the year 1719, Ziegenbalg finished the Bible in the Tamul tongue, having devoted *fourteen* years to the work. The peculiar interest taken by the king in this primary endeavour to evangelize the Hindoos, will appear from the following letters, addressed to the missionaries by his Majesty.

"GEORGE, by the Grace of God, King of Great Britain, France and Ireland, Defender of the Faith, &c. to the reverend and learned Bartholomew Ziegenbalgius and John Earnest Grundlerus, missionaries at Tranquebar in the East Indies.

"Reverend and beloved,

"Your letters dated the 20th of January of the present year, were most welcome to us; not only because the work undertaken by you of converting the heathen to the christian faith, doth, by the grace of God, prosper, but also because that, in this our kingdom, such a laudable zeal for the promotion of the gospel prevails.

"We pray you may be endued with health and strength of body, that you may long continue to fulfil your ministry with good success; of which, as we shall be rejoiced to hear, so you will always find us ready to succour you in whatever may tend to promote your work, and to excite your zeal. We assure you of the continuance of our royal favour.

"GEORGE R."

"Given at our Palace of Hampton Court, the 23rd of August, A. D. 1717, in the 4th year of our reign."

The king continued to cherish, with much solicitude, the interests of the mission, after the death of Ziegenbalgius; and in ten years from the date of the foregoing letter, a second was addressed to the members of the mission, by his Majesty.

"Reverend and beloved,

"From your letters dated Tranquebar, the 12th of September, 1725, which some time since came to hand, we received much pleasure; since by them we are informed, not only of your zealous exertions in the prosecution of the work committed to you, but also of the happy success which hath hitherto attended it, and which hath been graciously given of God.

"We return you thanks for these accounts, and it will be acceptable to us, if you continue to communicate whatever shall occur in the progress of your mission.

"In the mean time, we pray you may enjoy strength of body and mind for the long continuance of your labours in this good work, to the glory of God, and the promotion of christianity among the heathens; *that its perpetuity may not fail in generations to come.**

"GEORGE R."

"Given at our palace at St. James's, the 23d of February, 1727, in the 13th year of our reign."

But these royal epistles are not the only evangelic documents, of high authority, in the hands of the Hindoos. They are in possession of letters written by the Archbishop of Canterbury, of the same reign; † who supported the interests of the mission with unexampled liberality, affection, and zeal. These letters, which are many in number, are all written in the Latin language. The following is a translation of his Grace's first letter; which appears to have been written by him as President of the "Society for promoting Christian Knowledge."

"To Bartholomew Ziegenbalgius, and John Earnest Grundlerus, preachers of the christian faith, on the Coast of Coromandel.

"As often as I behold your letters, reverend brethren, addressed to the venerable society instituted for the promotion of the gospel, whose chief honour and ornament ye are; and as often as I contemplate the light of the gospel, either now first rising on the Indian nations, or after the intermission of some ages again revived, and as it were restored to its inheritance; I am constrained to magnify that singular goodness of God in visiting nations so remote; and to account you, my brethren, highly honoured, whose ministry it hath pleased him to employ in this pious work, to the glory of his name, and the salvation of so many millions of souls.

"Let others indulge in a ministry, if not idle, certainly less laborious, among christians at home. Let them enjoy in the bosom of the church, titles and honours,

* Niecampius. Hist. Miss. † Archbishop Wake.

obtained without labour and without danger. Your praise it will be (a praise of endless duration on earth, and followed by a just recompense in heaven) to have laboured in the vineyard which yourselves have planted; to have declared the name of Christ, where it was not known before: and through much peril and difficulty to have converted to the faith those among whom ye afterwards fulfilled your ministry. Your province, therefore, brethren, your office, I place before all dignities in the church. Let others be pontiffs, patriarchs, or popes; let them glitter in purple, in scarlet, or in gold; let them seek the admiration of the wondering multitude, and receive obeisance on the bended knee. Ye have acquired a better name than they, and a more sacred fame. And when that day shall arrive when the chief Shepherd shall give to every man *according to his work*, a greater reward shall be adjudged to you. Admitted into the glorious society of the prophets, evangelists, and apostles, ye, with them, shall shine like the sun among the lesser stars in the kingdom of your Father, for ever.

"Since then so great honour is now given unto you by all competent judges on earth, and since so great a reward is laid up for you in heaven, go forth with alacrity to that work, to the which the Holy Ghost hath called you. God hath already given to you an illustrious pledge of his favour, an increase not to be expected without the aid of his grace. Ye have begun happily, proceed with spirit. He, who hath carried you safely through the dangers of the seas to such a remote country, and who hath given you favour in the eyes of those whose countenance ye most desired; he who hath so liberally and unexpectedly ministered unto your wants, and who doth now daily add members to your church; he will continue to prosper your endeavours, and will subdue unto himself, by your means, the *whole continent of Oriental India.*

"O happy men! who, standing before the tribunal of Christ, shall exhibit so many nations converted to his faith by your preaching; happy men! to whom it shall be given to say before the assembly of the whole human race, 'Behold us, O Lord, and the children whom thou hast given us;' happy men! who being justified by the Saviour, shall receive in that day the reward of your labours, and also shall hear that glorious encomium, 'Well done, good and faithful servants, enter ye into the joy of your Lord.'

"May Almighty God graciously favour you and your labours, in all things. May he send to your aid fellow-labourers, such and as many as ye wish. May he increase the bounds of your churches. May he open the hearts of those to whom ye preach the gospel of Christ, that hearing you, they may receive life-giving faith. May he protect you and yours from all evils and dangers; and when ye arrive (may it be late) at the end of your course, may the same God, who hath called you to this work of the gospel, and hath preserved you in it, grant to you the reward of your labour, an incorruptible crown of glory.

"These are the fervent wishes and prayers of, venerable brethren,

"Your most faithful
Fellow-servant in Christ,
GULIELMUS CANT."

"From our Palace at Lambeth,
January 7, A. D. 1719."

Providence hath been pleased to grant the prayer of the king, "that the work might not fail in generations to come;" and the prophecy of his archbishop is likely to be fulfilled, that it should extend "over the whole continent of Oriental India."—After the first missionary Ziegenbalg had finished his course, he was followed by other learned and zealous men, upwards of fifty in number in the period of a hundred years, among whom were Schultz, Iænicke, Gericke, and Swartz, whose ministry has been continued in succession in different provinces, unto this time. The present state of the mission will appear by the following extract from the journal of the author's tour through these provinces.

"*Tranquebar*, 25*th August*, 1806.

"Tranquebar was the first scene of the Protestant mission in India. There are at present three missionaries here, superintending the Hindoo congregations. Yesterday I visited the church built by Ziegenbalg.

His body lies on one side of the altar, and that of his fellow missionary GRUNDLER on the other. Above are the epitaphs of both, written in Latin and engraved on plates of brass. The church was consecrated in 1718, and Ziegenbalg and his companion died in two years after. They laid the foundation for evangelizing India, and then departed, 'having finished the work which was given them to do.' I saw also the dwelling-house of Ziegenbalg, in the lower apartment of which the registers of the church are still kept. In these I found the name of the first heathen baptized by him, and recorded in his own hand-writing in the year 1707.—In Ziegenbalg's church, and from the pulpit where he stood, I first heard the gospel preached to a congregation of Hindoos, in their own tongue.—The missionaries told me that religion had suffered much in Tranquebar, of late years, from European infidelity. French principles had corrupted the Danes, and rendered them indifferent to their own religion, and therefore hostile to the conversion of the Hindoos. 'Religion,' said they, 'flourishes more among the natives of Tanjore, and in other provinces where there are few Europeans, than here or at Madras; for we find that European example, in the large towns, is the bane of christian instruction.'—One instance of hostility to the mission they mentioned as having occurred only a few weeks before my arrival. On the 9th of July, 1756, the native christians at Tranquebar celebrated a JUBILEE, in commemoration of the *fiftieth* year since the christian ministers brought the Bible from Europe. The present year, 1806, being the second 50th, preparations were made at Tranquebar for the second jubilee, on the 9th of last month; but the French principles preponderating in the government, they would not give it any public support; in consequence of which it was not observed with that solemnity which was intended. But in other places, where there were few Europeans, it was celebrated by the native christians with enthusiasm and every demonstration of joy. When I expressed my astonishment at this hostility, the aged missionary, Dr. John, said, 'I have always remarked that the disciples of Voltaire are the true enemies of missions, and that the enemies of missions are, in general, the disciples of Voltaire.' "

"*Tanjore*, 30*th August*, 1806.

"On my entering this province, I stopped an hour at a village near the road; and there I first heard the name of SWARTZ pronounced by a Hindoo. When I arrived at the capital, I waited on Major Blackburne, the British resident at the court of Tanjore, who informed me that the Rajah had appointed the next day at twelve o'clock to receive my visit. On the same day I went to Swartz's garden close to the christian village, where the Rev. Mr. Kohloff resides. Mr. Kohloff is the worthy successor of Mr. Swartz; and with him I found the Rev. Dr. John, and Mr. Horst, two other missionaries, who were on a visit to Mr. Kohloff.

"Next day I visited the Rajah of Tanjore, in company with Major Blackburne. When the first ceremonial was over, the Rajah conducted us to the grand saloon, which was adorned by the portraits of his ancestors; and immediately led me up to the portrait of Mr. Swartz. He then discoursed for a considerable time concerning 'that good man,' whom he ever revered as 'his father and guardian.' The Rajah speaks and writes English very intelligibly.—I smiled to see Swartz's picture amongst these Hindoo kings, and thought with myself that there are many who would think such a combination scarcely possible.—I then addressed the Rajah, and thanked him, in the name of the Church of England, for his kindness to the late Mr. Swartz, and to his successors, and particularly for his recent acts of benevolence to the christians residing within his provinces. The missionaries had just informed me that the Rajah had erected 'a college for Hindoos, Mahometans, and Christians;' in which provision was made for the instruction of '*fifty christian* children.' His highness is very desirous that I should visit this college, which is only about sixteen miles from the capital.—Having heard of the fame of the ancient Sanscrit, and Mahratta library of the kings of Tanjore, I requested his highness would present a catalogue of its volumes to the college of Fort-William; which he was pleased to do. It is voluminous, and written in the Mahratta character, for that is the proper language of the Tanjore court.

"In the evening I dined with the Resident, and the Rajah sent his band of music, consisting of eight or more *Vinas* with other instruments. The *Vina* or *Been*, is the ancient instrument which Sir William Jones has described in his interesting descant on the musical science of the Hindoos, in the Asiatic Researches, and the sight of which, he says, he found it so difficult to obtain in Northern India. The band played the English air of 'God save the King,' set to Mahratta words, and applied to the Maha Rajah, or great king of Tanjore. Two of the missionaries dined at the resident's house, together with some English officers. Mr. Kohloff informed me that Major Blackburne has promoted the interests of the mission by every means in his power. Major Blackburne is a man of superior attainments, amiable manners, and a hospitable disposition; and is well qualified for the important station he has long held, as English resident at this court.

"On the day following, I went to view the Hindoo temples, and saw the great BLACK BULL of Tanjore; it is said to be of one stone, hewn out of a rock of granite; and so large that the temple was built around it. While I surveyed it, I reflected on the multitude of natives, who, during the last hundred years, had turned away their eyes from this idol.—When I returned, I sat some hours with the missionaries, conversing on the general state of christianity in the provinces of Tanjore, Tritchinopoly, Madura, and Palamcottah. They want help; their vineyard is increased, and their labourers are decreased; they have had no supply from Germany in the room of Swartz, Iænicke, and Gericke; and they have no prospect of further supply, except from 'the Society for promoting Christian Knowledge;' who, they hope, will be able to send out English preachers to perpetuate the mission."

"*Tanjore, September* 2, 1806.

"Last Sunday and Monday were interesting days to me, at Tanjore. It being rumoured that a friend of the late Mr. Swartz had arrived, the people assembled from all quarters. On Sunday three sermons were preached in three different languages.—At eight o'clock we proceeded to the church built by Mr. Swartz within the Fort. From Mr. Swartz's pulpit I preached in English from Mark xiii. 10. 'And the gospel must first be published among all nations.' The English gentlemen here attended, civil and military, with the missionaries, catechists, and British soldiers.—After this service was ended, the congregation of Hindoos assembled in the same church, and filled the aisles and porches. The Tamul service commenced with some forms of prayer, in which all the congregation joined with loud fervour. A chapter of the Bible was then read, and a hymn of Luther's sung. After a short extempore prayer, during which the whole congregation knelt on the floor, the Rev. Dr. John delivered an animated discourse in the Tamul tongue, from these words, 'Jesus stood and cried, saying, If any man thirst, let him come to me and drink.'—As Mr. Whitefield, on his first going to Scotland, was surprised at the rustling of the leaves of the Bible, which took place immediately on his pronouncing his text (so different from any thing he had seen in his own country) so I was surprised here at the sound of the iron pen engraving the Palmyra leaf. Many persons had their *ollas* in their hands writing the sermon in Tamul short-hand. Mr. Kohloff assured me that some of the elder students and catechists will not lose a word of the preacher if he speak deliberately.* This, thought I, is more than some of the students at our English universities can do. This aptitude of the people to record the words of the preacher, renders it peculiarly necessary that 'the priests' lips should keep knowledge.' An old rule of the mission is, that the sermon of the morning should be read to the schools in the evening, by the catechist, from his Palmyra leaf.

"Another custom obtains among them which pleased me much. In the midst of the discourse the preacher sometimes puts a question to the congregation; who answer it without hesitation, in one voice. The object is to keep their attention awake, and the minister generally prompts the answer himself. Thus, suppose that

* It is well known that natives of Tanjore and Travancore can write fluently what is spoken deliberately. They do not look much at their ollas while writing. The fibre of the leaf guides the pen.

he is saying, 'My dear brethren, it is true that your profession of the faith of Christ is attended with some reproach, and that you have lost your cast with the Brahmins; but your case is not peculiar. The man of the world is the man of cast in Europe; and he despises the humble and devout disciple of Christ, even as your Brahmin contemns the *Sooder*. But, thus it hath been from the beginning. Every faithful christian must lose cast for the gospel; even as Christ himself, the forerunner, made himself of no reputation, and was despised and rejected of men. In like manner you will be despised; but be of good cheer, and say, Though we have lost our cast and inheritance amongst men, we shall receive in heaven a new name and a better inheritance, through Jesus Christ our Lord.' He then adds, 'What, my beloved brethren, shall you obtain in heaven?' They answer, 'a new name and a better inheritance, through Jesus Christ our Lord.' It is impossible for a stranger not to be affected with this scene.—This custom is deduced from Ziegenbalg, who proved its use by long experience.

"After the sermon was ended, I returned with the missionaries into the vestry or library of the church. Here I was introduced to the elders and catechists of the congregation; among others came SATTIANADEN, the Hindoo preacher, one of whose sermons was published in England some years ago, by the Society for promoting Christian Knowledge. He is now advanced in years, and his black locks have grown grey. As I returned from the church, I saw the christian families going back in crowds to the country, and the boys looking at their ollas. What a contrast, thought I, is this to the scene at Juggernaut! Here there is becoming dress, humane affections, and rational discourse. I see here no skulls, no self-torture, no self-murder, no dogs and vultures tearing human flesh! Here the christian virtues are found in exercise by the feeble-minded Hindoo, in a vigour and purity which will surprise those who have never known the native character but under the greatest disadvantages, as in Bengal. It certainly surprised myself; and when I reflected on the moral conduct, upright dealing, and decorous manners of the native christians of Tanjore, I found in my breast a new evidence of the peculiar excellence and benign influence of the christian faith.

"At four o'clock in the afternoon, we attended divine service at the chapel in the Mission Garden out of the Fort. The Rev. Mr. Horst preached in the *Portuguese* language. The organ here accompanied the voice in singing. I sat on a granite stone which covered the grave of Swartz. The epitaph is in English verse, written by the present Rajah, and signed by him, 'Serfogee.'—In the evening Mr. Kohloff presided at the exercise in the schools: on which occasion the Tamul sermon was repeated, and the boys' ollas examined.

"In consequence of my having expressed a wish to hear Sattianaden preach, Mr. Kohloff had given notice that there would be divine service next day, Monday; accordingly the chapel in Swartz's garden was crowded at an early hour. Sattianaden delivered his discourse in the Tamul language, with much natural eloquence, and with visible effect. His subject was the 'Marvellous Light.' He first described the pagan darkness, then the light of Ziegenbalg, then the light of Swartz, and then the heavenly light, 'when there shall be no more need of the light of the sun, or of the moon.' In quoting a passage from scripture, he desired a lower minister to read it, listening to it as to a record; and then proceeded to the illustration. The responses by the audience were more frequently called for than in the former sermon. He concluded with praying fervently for the glory and prosperity of the church of England.—After the sermon, I went up to Sattianaden, and the old christians who had known Swartz came around us. They were anxious to hear something of the progress of christianity in the North of India. They said they had heard good news from Bengal. I told them that the news was good, but that Bengal was exactly a hundred years behind Tanjore.

"I have had long conversations with the missionaries, relating to the present circumstances of the Tanjore mission. It is in a languishing state at this moment, in consequence of the war on the continent of Europe. Two of its sources have dried up, the Royal College at *Copenhagen*, and the Orphan-house at *Halle*, in Germany. Their remaining resource from Europe is the stipend of

'The Society for promoting Christian Knowledge;' whom they never mention but with emotions of gratitude and affection. But this supply is by no means commensurate with the increasing number of their churches and schools. The chief support of the mission is derived from itself. Mr. Swartz had in his life time acquired a considerable property, through the kindness of the English government and of the native princes. When he was dying, he said, 'Let the cause of Christ be my heir.' When his colleague, the pious Gericke, was departing, he also bequeathed his property to the mission. And now Mr. Kohloff gives from his private funds an annual sum; not that he can well afford it; but the mission is so extended, that he gives it, he told me, to preserve the new and remote congregations in *existence*. He stated that there were upwards of ten thousand Protestant christians belonging to the Tanjore and Tinavelly districts alone, who had not among them one complete copy of the Bible; and that not one christian, perhaps, in a hundred had a New Testament; and yet there are some copies of the Tamul scriptures still to be sold at Tranquebar; but the poor natives cannot afford to purchase them. When I mentioned the designs of the Bible Society in England, they received the tidings with very sensible emotions of thankfulness. Mr. Horst said, if only every tenth person were to obtain a copy of the scriptures, it would be an event long to be remembered in Tanjore. They lamented much that they were destitute of the aid of a printing-press, and represented to me that the progress of christianity had been materially retarded of late years by the want of that important auxiliary. They have petitioned the Society for promoting Christian Knowledge to send them one. They justly observed, if you can no longer send us missionaries to preach the gospel, send us the means of printing the gospel.* The Tranquebar mission and the Madras mission have both possessed printing-presses for a long period; by the means of which they have

* The Brahmins in Tanjore have procured a press, "which they dedicate (say the missionaries in their last letter) to the glory of their gods;" but the missionaries, who first introduced the civilization of christianity at the Tanjore capital, are still without one. Printing is certainly the legitimate instrument of the christian for the promulgation of christianity. We Protestants have put it into the hands of the Brahmins, and we ought to see to it, that the teachers of our own religion are possessed of an equal advantage.

been extensively useful in distributing the scriptures and religious publications in several languages. The mission press at Tranquebar may be said to have been the fountain of all the good that was done in India during the last century. It was established by Ziegenbalg. From this press, in conjunction with that at *Halle* in Germany, have proceeded volumes in Arabic, Syriac, Hindostanee, Tamul, Telinga, Portuguese, Danish, and English. I have in my possession the Psalms of David in the *Hindostanee* language, printed in the Arabic character; and the History of Christ in *Syriac*, intended, probably, for the Syro-Romish christians on the sea-coast of Travancore, whom a Danish missionary once visited, both of which volumes were edited by the missionaries of Tranquebar. There is also in Swartz's library at Tanjore, a Grammar of the *Hindostanee* language, in quarto, published at the same press; an important fact which was not known at the college of Fort-William, when Professor Gilchrist commenced his useful labours in that language."

"*Tanjore, Sept*. 3, 1806.

"Before I left the capital of Tanjore, the Rajah was pleased to honour me with a second audience. On this occasion he presented to me a portrait of himself, a very striking likeness, painted by a Hindoo artist at the Tanjore court.*—The missionary, Dr. John, accompanied me to the palace. The Rajah received him with much kindness, and presented to him a piece of gold cloth. Of the resident missionary, Mr. Kohloff, whom the Rajah sees frequently, he spoke to me in terms of high approbation. This cannot be very agreeable to the Brahmins; but the Rajah, though he yet professes the Brahminical religion, is no longer obedient to the dictates of the Brahmins, and they are compelled to admit his superior attainments in knowledge.—I passed the chief part of this morning in looking over Mr. Swartz's manuscripts and books; and when I was coming away Mr. Kohloff presented to me a Hebrew

* It is now placed in the public library of the University of Cambridge.

Psalter, which had been Mr. Swartz's companion for fifty years; also a brass lamp which he had got first when a student at the college of Halle, and had used in his lucubrations to the time of his death; for Mr. Swartz *seldom preached to the natives without previous study*. I thought I saw the image of Swartz in his successor. Mr. Kohloff is a man of great simplicity of manners, of meek deportment, and of ardent zeal in the cause of revealed religion, and of humanity. He walked with me through the christian village close to his house; and I was much pleased to see the affectionate respect of the people towards him; the young people of both sexes coming forward from the doors on both sides, to salute him and receive his benediction."*

"*September 4th.* 1806.

"Leaving Tanjore, I passed through the woods inhabited by the Collaries (or thieves) now humanized by christianity. When they understood who I was, they followed me on the road, stating their destitute condition, in regard to religious instruction. They were

* That I may give to those who are interested in the promotion of christianity in the East, a more just view of the character of Swartz's successor, the Rev. Mr. Kohloff, I shall subjoin an extract of a letter which I have since received from the Rev. Mr. Horst.

"TANJORE, Sept. 24, 1807.

"The Rev. Mr. Kohloff is sometimes rather weak, on account of so many and various cares that assail him without ceasing. He provides for the wants of this and the Southern Missions (Tritchinopoly excepted) by disbursing annually upwards of one thousand pagodas (about £250 sterling) out of his private purse, partly to make up the difference between the income and expenditure of this and the Southern Mission (of which I annex an abstract) and the rest in assisting the deserving poor, without regard to religion; and for various pious uses. To him, as arbitrator and father, apply all christians that are at variance, disturbed from without or from within, out of service or distressed; for most of our christians will do any thing rather than go to law.

"All these heterogeneous, but, to a missionary at Tanjore, unavoidable avocations, joined to the ordinary duties of his station, exercise his mind early and late; and if he be not of a robust constitution, will undermine his health at last. Happily, several neighbouring churches and new congregations, belonging to the mission of Tanjore, afford Mr. Kohloff frequent opportunities to relax his mind, and to recruit his health and spirits, by making occasional short excursions to see these new christians, who were professed thieves only a few years ago, and many of them are now an honour to the christian profession, and industrious peasants. It is pleasing to behold the anxiety with which a great number of our christian children inquire at such times when their father will return; and how they run several miles to meet him with shouts and clapping of hands, and hymns of thanks to God, as soon as they discern his palankeen at a distance."

clamorous for Bibles; they supplicated for teachers.—'We don't want bread or money from you,' said they, 'but we want the word of God.'—Now, thought I, whose duty is it to attend to the moral wants of this people? Is it that of the English nation, or of some other nation?"

"*Tritchinopoly, September 5th.*

"The first church built by Swartz is at this place; it is called Christ's Church, and is a large building, capable of containing, perhaps, two hundred people. The aged missionary, the Rev. Mr. Pohle, presides over this church, and over the native congregations at this place. Christianity flourishes; but I found that here, as at other places, there is a 'famine of Bibles.' The jubilee was celebrated on the 9th of July, being the hundredth year from the arrival of the messengers of the gospel. On this occasion their venerable pastor preached from Matth. xxviii. 19. 'Go ye therefore, and teach all nations, baptizing them in the name of the Father, and of the Son, and of the Holy Ghost.'—At this station, there are about a thousand English troops. Mr. Pohle being a German, does not speak English very well; but he is reverenced for his piety by the English; and both officers and men *are glad to hear the religion of their country preached in any way.*—On the Sunday morning, I preached in Christ's Church to a full assembly, from these words, 'For we have seen his Star in the East, and are come to worship him.' Indeed what I had seen in these provinces rendered this text the most appropriate I could select. Next day some of the English soldiers came to me, desiring to know how they might procure Bibles. 'It is a delightful thing,' said one of them, 'to hear our own religion preached by our own countryman.' I am informed that there are at this time above twenty English regiments in India, and that not one of them has a chaplain. The men live without religion, and then they bury each other. O England, England, it is not for thine own goodness that Providence giveth thee the treasures of India!

"I proceeded hence to visit the christian churches in the provinces of Madura, and Tinavelly."

The friends of christianity in India have had it in their power to afford some aid to the christian churches in Tanjore. On the 1st of January of the present year (1810,) the Rev. Mr. Brown preached a sermon at Calcutta, in which he represented the petition of the Hindoos for Bibles. A plain statement of the fact was sufficient to open the hearts of the public. A subscription was immediately set on foot, and Lieut.-General Hewitt, commander-in-chief, then deputy governor in Bengal, subscribed £250. The chief officers of government, and the principal inhabitants of Calcutta, raised the subscription, in a few days, to the sum of £1000 sterling. Instructions were sent to Mr. Kohloff, to buy up all the copies of the Tamul scriptures; to distribute them at a small price amongst the natives, and to order a new edition to be printed off without loss of time.*

VERSIONS OF THE SCRIPTURES FOR THE HINDOOS.

HAVING now seen what the Hindoos are in their state of idolatry, as at Juggernaut, and in Bengal; and what they may become under the influence of christianity, as at Tranquebar, Tritchinopoly, and Tanjore; it remains to give some account of the translation of the scriptures into the languages of the Hindoos.

There are five principal languages spoken by Hindoos in countries subject to the British empire. These are, the *Hindostanee,* which pervades Hindostan generally; and the four languages of the four great provinces, viz. the *Bengalee,* for the province of Bengal; the *Telinga,* for the Northern Sircars; the *Tamul,* for Coromandel,

* The chief names in this subscription, besides that of General Hewitt, were Sir John Royds, Sir W. Borroughs, John Lumsden, esq., George Udney, esq., J. H. Harrington, esq., Sir John D'Oyley, Colonel Carey, John Thornhill, esq., R. C. Plowden. esq., Thos. Hayes, esq., W. Egerton, esq., &c. &c.

Thus, while we are disputing in England whether the Bible ought to be given to the Hindoos, the deputy governor in Bengal, the members of the supreme council, and of the supreme court of judicature, and the chief officers of the government, after perusing the information concerning the state of India sent from this country, are satisfied that it is an important duty, and a christian obligation.

and the Carnatic; and the *Malayalim*, or *Malabar*, for the coast of Malabar and Travancore.

Of these five languages, there are two, into which the scriptures are already translated; the *Tamul*, by the Danish missionaries in the last century; and the *Bengalee*, by the Baptist missionaries from England. The remaining three languages are in progress of translation; the *Hindostanee*, by the Rev. Henry Martin, B. A. Chaplain in Bengal; * the *Malabar*, by Mar Dionysius, bishop of the Syrian christians in Travancore, both of which translations will be noticed more particularly hereafter; and the *Telinga*, by Ananda Rayer, a Telinga Brahmin, by birth a Mahratta, under the superintendence of Mr. Augustus Desgranges at Vizagapatam, a missionary belonging to the London society.

Ananda Rayer, a Brahmin of high cast, was lately converted to the christian faith, and has given undoubted proofs of the serious impression of its principles on his heart. † It is remarkable that versions of the scriptures should be now preparing for the Mahomedans and

* It was before mentioned that the gospels were translated into Hindostanee, and part of them printed in the college of Fort-William. Another version has since been published by the Baptist missionaries. The Hindostanee being spoken over such extensive regions, varies much in its dialects.

† The account of Ananda Rayer's conversion is given by the Rev. Dr. John, the aged missionary at Tranquebar, in a letter to Mr. Desgranges. This Brahmin applied (as many Brahmins and other Hindoos constantly do) to an older Brahmin of some fame for sanctity, to know "what he should do that he might be saved?" The old Brahmin told him, that "he must repeat a certain prayer four lack of times:" that is, 400,000 times. This he performed in a pagoda, in six months; and added many painful ceremonies. But finding no comfort or peace from these external rites, he went to a Romish priest, and asked him if he knew what was the true religion? The priest gave him some christian books in the Telinga language; and, after a long investigation of christianity, the inquiring Hindoo had no doubt remaining on his mind, that "Christ was the Saviour of the world." But he was not satisfied with the Romish worship in many points; he disliked the adoration of images, and other superstitions; and having heard from the priests themselves, that the Protestant christians at Tanjore and Tranquebar, professed to have a purer faith, and had got the Bible translated, and worshipped no images; he visited Dr. John, and the other missionaries at Tranquebar, where he remained four months, conversing, says Dr. John, "almost every day with me," and examining the holy scriptures. He soon acquired the Tamul language (which has affinity with the Telinga) that he might read the Tamul translation; and he finally became a member of the Protestant church.

The missionaries at Vizagapatam being in want of a learned Telinga scholar, to assist them in a translation of the scriptures into the Telinga language, Dr. John recommended Ananda Rayer; "for he was averse," says he, "to undertake any worldly employment, and had a great desire to be useful to his brethren of the Telinga nation." The reverend missionary concludes thus: "What Jesus Christ hath required of his followers, this man hath literally done; he hath left father, mother, sisters, and brothers, and houses, and lands, for the gospel's sake."—See Dr. John's letter, dated 29th January, 1808, communicated to the Bible Society, by the Rev. Mr. Brown.

Hindoos, by their own converted countrymen; namely, the Persian and Arabic versions, by SABAT the Arabian; and the Telinga version by ANANDA RAYER, the Telinga Brahmin. The latter has translated the four Gospels, and the Acts of the Apostles. The progress of Sabat in his translations will be noticed hereafter.

THE CEYLONESE.

IN the island of Ceylon, the population under the British government amounts, according to the best authorities, to upwards of a million and a half; and one-third is supposed to profess christianity. This population was divided by the Dutch, while they had possession of the island, into 240 church-ships, and three native schoolmasters were appointed to each church-ship. The Dutch government never gave an official appointment to any native who was not a christian; a distinction which was ever considered by them as a wise policy, as well as a christian duty, and which is continued by his majesty's government in Ceylon. Perhaps it is not generally known in England that our Bengal and Madras governments do not patronise the native christians. They give official appointments to Mahomedans and Hindoos generally in *preference* to natives professing christianity. The chief argument for the retention of this system is *precedent;* it was the practice of the first settlers. But it has been often observed that what might be proper or necessary in a *factory*, may not be tolerable in a great *empire*. It is certain that this system confirms prejudice, exposes our religion to contempt in the eyes of the natives, and precludes every ray of hope of the future prevalence of christianity at the seats of government.

"*Jaffna-patam, in Ceylon, Sept*. 27, 1806.

"From the Hindoo temple of Ramisseram, I crossed over to Ceylon, keeping close to Adam's bridge. I was surprised to find that all the boatmen were christians of Ceylon. I asked the helmsman what religion the English professed, who now governed the island. He said he could not tell, only that they were, not of the Portuguese or Dutch religion. I was not so much surprised at his ignorance afterwards, as I was at the time.

"I have had the pleasure to meet here with Alexander Johnstone, esq.* of the supreme court of judicature, who is on the circuit; a man of large and liberal views, the friend of learning and of christianity. He is well acquainted with the language of the country, and with the history of the island; and his professional pursuits afford him a particular knowledge of its present state; so that his communications are truly valuable.—It will be scarcely believed in England, that there are here Protestant churches under the king's government, which are without ministers. In the time of BALDÆUS, the Dutch preacher and historian, there were *thirty-two* christian churches in the province of Jaffna alone. At this time there is not one Protestant European minister in the whole province. I ought to except Mr. Palm, a solitary missionary, who has been sent out by the London Society, and receives some stipend from the British government. I visited Mr. Palm, at his residence, a few miles from the town of Jaffna. He is prosecuting the study of the *Tamul* language; for that is the language of this part of Ceylon, from its proximity to the Tamul continent. Mrs. Palm has made as great progress in the language as her husband, and is extremely active in the instruction of the native women and children. I asked her if she had no wish to return to Europe after living so long among the uncivilized Cingalese. No, she said; she was 'all the day long happy in the communication of knowledge.' Mr. Palm has taken possession of the old Protestant church of Tilly-Pally. By reference to the history, I found it was the church in which Baldæus himself preached (as he himself mentions) to a congregation of two thousand natives, for a view of the church is given in his work. Most of those handsome churches, of which views are given in the plates of Baldæus' history, are now in ruins. Even in the town and fort of Jaffna, where there is a spacious edifice for divine worship, and a respectable society of English and Dutch inhabitants, no clergyman has been yet appointed. The only Protestant preacher in the town of Jaffna is *Christian*

* Now Sir Alexander Johnstone, Chief-Justice of Ceylon.

David, a Hindoo catechist sent over by the mission of Tranquebar. His chief ministrations are in the Tamul tongue; but he sometimes preaches in the English language, which he speaks with tolerable propriety; and the Dutch and English resort to hear him. I went with the rest to his church; when he delivered extempore a very excellent discourse, which his present majesty George the Third would not have disdained to hear. And this Hindoo supports the interests of the English church in the province of Jaffna. The Dutch ministers who formerly officiated here, have gone to Batavia or to Europe. The whole district is now in the hands of the Romish priests from the college Goa; who perceiving the indifference of the English nation to their own religion, have assumed quiet and undisturbed possession of the land. And the English government justly preferring the Romish superstition to the worship of the idol *Boodha,* thinks it right to countenance the catholic religion in Ceylon. But whenever our church shall direct her attention to the promotion of christianity in the east, I know of no place which is more worthy of her labour, than the old Protestant vineyard of Jaffna Patam. The scriptures are already prepared in the Tamul language. The language of the rest of Ceylon is the *Cingalese,* or *Ceylonese.*"

"*Columbo, in Ceylon,* 10*th March,* 1808.

"—— I find that the south part of the island is in much the same state as the north, in regard to christian instruction. There are but two English clergymen in the whole island. 'What wonder,' said a Romish priest to me, 'that your nation should be so little interested about the conversion of the pagans to christianity, when it does not even give teachers to its own subjects who are already christians?' I was not surprised to hear that great numbers of the Protestants every year go back to idolatry. Being destitute of a head to take cognizance of their state, they apostatise to *Boodha,* as the Israelites turned to *Baal* and *Ashteroth.* It is perhaps true that the religion of Christ has never been so disgraced in any age of the church, as it has been lately, by our official neglect of the Protestant church in Ceylon.

"I passed the day at Mount Lavinia, the country residence of General Maitland, the governor of Ceylon; and had some conversation with his Excellency on the religious state of the country. He desired I would commit to writing, and leave with him, a memorandum of inquiries which I wished should be made on subjects relating to the former prevalence of the Protestant religion in the island, and the means of reviving and establishing it once more. His Excellency expressed his conviction that some ecclesiastical establishment ought to be given to Ceylon; as had been given to other colonies of his Majesty in America and the West Indies. He asked what was the cause of the delay in giving an ecclesiastical establishment to the continent of India. I told him I supposed the chief cause was the mixed government of our Indian empire. It was said to be a question at home, who ought to originate it. Had there been no revolution in Europe to distract the attention of the nation, and had Mr. Pitt lived, many things of a grand and arduous character would have been done which are yet left undone.—There are now three missionaries of the London Society established in three different parts of the island. It gave me great pleasure to find that General Maitland, and the senior chaplain at Columbo, the honourable Mr. Twisleton, had afforded their patronage in the most liberal manner to these useful teachers. Government has allowed to each of them an annual stipend.—In returning from the country, I passed through the groves of CINNAMON, which extend nearly a mile in length. Ceylon is believed by some of the easterns, both Mahomedans and Hindoos, to have been the residence of the first man (for the Hindoos have a first man, and a garden of Eden, as well as the christians); because it abounds in 'trees pleasant to the eyes, and good for food;' and is famous for its rare metals and precious stones. 'There is gold, bdellium, and the onyx-stone.' The rocky ridge which connects this happy island with the main land, is called Adam's Bridge; the lofty mountain in the middle of the island, every where visible, is called Adam's Peak; and there is a sepulchre of immense length, which they call Abel's

Tomb. All these names were given many ages before the introduction of christianity from Europe.—The cinnamon trees love a sandy soil. The surface of the ground appeared to be entirely *sand*. I thought it wonderful that the most valuable of all trees should grow in luxuriance in such an arid soil without human culture. I compared them in my mind to the Ceylon christians in their present state, who are left to flourish by themselves under the blessing of heaven, without those external and rational aids which have been divinely appointed to nourish the church of Christ."

"*Columbo, 11th March,* 1808.

"I have conversed with intelligent persons on the means of translating the scriptures into the Cingalese language. The whole of the New Testament has been translated, but only three books of the Old Testament. But even this portion has been translated almost in vain; for there is no supply of books for the use of the people. I reflected with astonishment on the fact, that there are by computation 500,000 natives in Ceylon professing christianity, and that there should not be one complete copy of the holy scriptures in the vernacular tongue. Samuel Tolfry, esq., head of a civil department in Columbo, is a good Cingalese scholar, and is now engaged in compiling a Cingalese dictionary. I proposed to him to undertake the completion of the Cingalese Version; which is easily practicable, as there are many learned Cingalese christians in Columbo. He professed himself ready to engage in the work, provided he should receive the sanction of the government. I mentioned to him what had passed in my conversation with General Maitland, and his excellency's favourable sentiments on the subject; and added that a correspondence would be immediately commenced with him from Calcutta concerning the work, and funds apportioned for the execution of it. Alexander Johnstone, esq., who is now in Columbo, has furnished me with his sentiments on the best means of reviving and maintaining the Protestant interest in Ceylon. Did his professional avocations permit, Mr.

Johnstone is himself the fit person to superintend the translation and printing of the scriptures. It is a proof of the interest which this gentleman takes in the progress of christian knowledge, that he hath caused Bishop Porteus's Evidences of Christianity to be translated into the Cingalese tongue, for distribution among the natives.

THE MALAYS.

A NEW empire has been added to Great Britain in the east, which may be called her Malay Empire. The extensive dominion of the Dutch in the Indian Ocean, is devolving upon the English; and it may be expected that Britain will soon be mistress of the whole of the MALAYAN ARCHIPELAGO. But as we increase our territories, we increase our obligations. Our duties to our Hindoo empire have been long enough the subject of discussion: let us now turn our attention to the obligations which we owe to our Malay empire. We are now about to take possession of islands, peopled by numbers of Protestant christians; for in every island where the Dutch established their government, they endeavoured to convert the natives to christianity, and they were successful. Those amongst us who would recommend that the evangelization of barbarous nations should be deferred "till a more convenient season" will have no opportunity of offering the advice in regard to some of these islands; for, behold, the natives are christians already. They profess the religion of the Bible. Let it be our endeavour then to do more justice to these our new Protestant subjects than we have done to the christians of Ceylon. We have less excuse in the present instance, for the Malay scriptures are already translated to our hands. What a noble field here opens to the view of the "Society for promoting Christian Knowledge," and of the Bible Society! Here there is ample room for a praise-worthy emulation, and for the utmost exercise of their benevolent exertions. One hundred thousand Malay Bibles will not suffice to supply the Malay christians.

The sacred scriptures were translated by the Dutch, into the eastern Malay; * for that is the general language of their extensive dominions in the Indian sea. But the eastern Malay is different from the western Malay, or that of Sumatra. In the college of Fort-William, Thomas Jarrett, esq. of the honourable Company's civil service, was preparing a version of the scriptures in the western Malay; for which undertaking he was well qualified, having resided twelve years in Sumatra. When the progress of the Biblical translations was interrupted in the college, Mr. Jarrett prosecuted the work, after his return to Madras. He has had, as an assistant in the design, a learned Malay of the rank of Rajah in his own country, who came from Sumatra for the purpose. Mr. Jarrett has also made considerable progress in compiling a copious Malay dictionary, which he commenced before he left the island. His labour, it is to be hoped, will not be lost to the public; for the Malay language is daily increasing in its importance to the British nation.

Prince of Wales' Island, or, as it is called by the natives, Penang, or Pulo Penang, that is, the island Penang, is the capital of our Malay territories, and is the proper place for the cultivation of the Malay language, being situated close to the main land of Malacca. As there is a college in Bengal for instructing the English in the languages of the continent of Hindostan, it is equally expedient that there should be an institution in Penang for the cultivation of the Malay tongue, and of the various dialects of our insular possessions. The Dutch attended to this object in the very infancy of their empire. Besides, it is probable that Penang will, in the progress of eastern civilization, become the great emporium of Asiatic commerce. Its sudden elevation, is a prognostic of its future celebrity. It is situated on what may be called, "the high way," in which ships sail from either hemisphere; and is the very centre of British navigation in the east. The author resided on this island for about a month, and was greatly surprised at the variety of languages which are spoken, and at the

* A complete version of the Malay Bible was published in the Arabic character at Batavia, in 5 vols. 8vo. in 1758, under the direction of Jacob Mossel, Govenor-General of the Dutch possessions in the East Indies.

different races of men who present themselves to view in this infant settlement. The merchants are chiefly of the Malay, and Indo-Chinese nations. John Shaw, esq. was prosecuting the study of the eastern Malay language, when I visited the island, and has since published a considerable portion of a Malay grammar.

The author who chiefly claims our notice in regard to the Malay regions is J. C. Leyden, M. D. professor of Hindostanee in the college of Fort-William. To him the learned world is indebted for "a Dissertation on the languages and literature of the Indo-Chinese nations," just published in the Asiatic Researches, in which he illuminates a very dark subject, and opens a new view to Great Britain of her insular possessions in Asia. Dr. Leyden takes the lead in this most useful science, in the east, being possessed of very rare talents for general philology, which he has applied almost suddenly, and with admirable effect, to the Oriental languages. If this erudite scholar should prosecute his researches for some years to come, with equal assiduity and success, he will promote, in the most effectual manner, the general civilization of the east, by opening the way for the future exertions of christian teachers, and preparing them for the study of languages, the names of which are not yet known in Europe.

Penang and the neighbouring settlement of Malacca, are most favourable stations for the study of the various dialects of the Malay and Chinese languages; and for pouring forth from the press useful works for the civilization of maritime and Austral Asia. Every week, boats of different nations are ready to carry off every thing that is printed to their respective regions. The author found here a general spirit of inquiry, a communicative disposition, and an unusual thirst for knowledge; for the civilities of commerce have a tendency to weaken prejudice and superstition among barbarous tribes.

Although the Dutch introduced christianity on every island where they established a government, yet the greater part of the Malay islands are involved in darkness. The natives are of three general casts, Pagans, Mahomedans, and Chinese. The Mahomedans chiefly inhabit the shores, and the Pagans the interior parts of the islands. The barbarism of the interior nations in

Sumatra, Borneo, and other islands, almost exceeds belief. Marsden, in his history of Sumatra, had informed us that it was usual with the natives of the interior, called the Batta tribes, to kill and eat their criminals, and prisoners of war; but the researches of Dr. Leyden have led to the discovery that they sometimes sacrifice their own relations. "They themselves declare," says he, "that they frequently eat their own relations when aged and infirm; and that not so much to gratify their appetite, as to perform a pious ceremony. Thus, when a man becomes infirm and weary of the world, he is said to invite his own children to eat him in the season when salt and limes are cheapest. He then ascends a tree, round which his friends and offspring assemble, and as they shake the tree, join in a funeral dirge, the import of which is, 'The season is come, the fruit is ripe, and it must descend.' The victim descends, and those that are nearest and dearest to him deprive him of life and devour his remains in a solemn banquet."*

These cannibals inhabit the interior of the island of Sumatra, on the shore of which is the English settlement, Bencoolen, or Fort-Marlborough. We have been settled there for a long period, and trade with the inhabitants for their spices. In return for the *pepper* which the natives give us, it would well become our character as a christian nation, were we now, at length, to offer them the *New Testament*.

Another description of barbarians in the eastern isles, are the *Haraforas*, called by the Dutch, the *Alfoers*. They are to be found in almost all the larger islands. "In their manners," says Dr. Leyden, "the most singular feature is the necessity imposed on every person of, some time in his life, imbruing his hands in human blood; and, in general, among all their tribes, no person is permitted to marry, till he can shew the skull of a man whom he has slaughtered. They eat the flesh of their enemies like the *Battas*, and drink out of their skulls; and the ornaments of their houses are human skulls and teeth."† When the author was at Pulo Penang, he himself saw a chief of the Malay tribe who had a staff, on the head of which was a bushy lock of human hair;

* Asiatic Researches, vol. X. p. 203. † Ibid. p. 217.

which he said he had cut from the head of his enemy whom he had killed.

The author has mentioned the foregoing circumstances to shew what paganism is in its natural state, and to awaken some desire of civilizing a people, who are now so accessible to us. Some philosophers of the school of Voltaire and Gibbon, have been extravagant in their eulogium of man in a state of nature, or in some other state DEVOID of christianity; and it is to be lamented that some *christian* writers have tried of late to draw the same picture. But paganism, in its best estate, is well described by one line of the poet:

Monstrum, horrendum, informe, ingens cui LUMEN ademptum. VIRG.

No quarter of the globe promises to be more auspicious to christian missions than the Malayan Archipelago. In regard to the probable success of our endeavours, the Dutch have already shewn *what is practicable*. The natives are of different casts, and are a divided people. The communication is easy from island to island; our own ships are continually plying on their shores. The China fleets pass through twice or oftener every year; and with most of the islands we have intercourse by what is called in India, the country trade. And now there will be, of course, an English government established in each of the conquered islands in lieu of the Dutch.

The Mahomedans found it easy to translate the Koran into the languages of *Java*, and of the *Celebes;* but the sacred scriptures are not yet translated into *either* of these languages. The proper language of Java is different from the Malay of the city of Batavia. The language of the Celebes is called the Bugis, or Bouguese.* The natives of Celebes are distinguished for their vigour of mind and strength of body; and are acknowledged to be the first of the *Orang Timor,* or eastern men. Literature was formerly cultivated among them. Dr. Leyden enumerates fifty-three different volumes. "Their songs," says he, "and romances are famous among all the islands of the east." Their language extends to other islands; for they formerly carried their conquests

* Lord Minto notices in his speech to the college of Fort-William, that Thomas Raffles, esq., secretary to the government in Prince of Wales' Island, is employed in compiling a code of Malay laws, in the Malay, and Bouguese languages.

beyond the Moluccas. The man who shall first translate the Bible into the language of the Celebes, will probably be read by as many islanders as have read the translation of Wickliffe. Let us consider how long these nations have waited for christian instruction, and contemplate the words of the prophecy, "The isles shall wait for HIS Law." Is. xlii. 4.

The facilities for civilizing the Malayan isles are certainly very great; and these facilities are our strongest encouragement to make the attempt. Both in our translation of the scriptures and in missions to the heathen, we should avoid as much as possible what may be called *enterprise*. Let us follow the path that is easy and secure, and make use of those means which are already afforded to us by providence. Thus the most valuable and important translation of the scriptures in the present circumstances, will be that for which a people are already prepared, such as the Malayalim, the Cingalese, and Malay. And the most judiciously planned missions will be those where there is a prospect of personal security to the teachers; and where there are, judging from human probabilities, the greatest facilities for the conversion of the people.

THE SYRIAN CHRISTIANS IN INDIA.

THE Syrian christians inhabit the interior of Travancore and Malabar, in the south of India; and have been settled there from the early ages of christianity. The first notices of this ancient people in recent times are to be found in the Portuguese histories. When Vasco de Gama arrived at Cochin on the coast of Malabar, in the year 1503, he saw the sceptre of the christian king; for the Syrian christians had formerly regal power in Malay-Ala.* The name or title of their last king was Beliarte; and he dying without issue, the dominion devolved on the king of Cochin and Diamper.

* Malay-ala is the proper name for the whole country of Travancore and Malabar, comprehending the territory between the mountains and the sea, from Cape Comorin to Cape Illi or Dilly. The language of these extensive regions is called Malayalim, and sometimes Malabar. We shall use the word Malabar, as being of easier pronunciation.

When the Portuguese arrived, they were agreeably surprised to find upwards of a hundred christian churches on the coast of Malabar. But when they became acquainted with the purity and simplicity of their worship, they were offended. "These churches," said the Portuguese, "belong to the Pope."—"Who is the Pope?" said the natives, "we never heard of him." The European priests were yet more alarmed, when they found that these Hindoo Christians maintained the order and discipline of a regular church under episcopal jurisdiction; and that, for 1300 years past they had enjoyed a succession of bishops appointed by the patriarch of Antioch. "We," said they, "are of the true faith, whatever you from the west may be; for we come from the place where the followers of Christ were first called christians."

When the power of the Portuguese became sufficient for their purpose, they invaded these tranquil churches, siezed some of the clergy, and devoted them to the death of heretics. Then the inhabitants heard for the first time that there was a place called the *Inquisition;* and that its fires had been lately lighted at Goa, near their own land. But the Portuguese, finding that the people were resolute in defending their ancient faith, began to try more conciliatory measures. They seized the Syrian bishop, Mar Joseph, and sent him prisoner to Lisbon; and then convened a synod at one of the Syrian churches called Diamper, near Cochin, at which the Romish archbishop Menezes presided. At this compulsory synod, 150 of the Syrian clergy appeared. They were accused of the following practices and opinions, "That they had married wives; that they owned but two sacraments, baptism and the Lord's supper; that they neither invoked saints, nor worshipped images, nor believed in purgatory; and that they had no other orders or names of dignity in the church, than bishop, priest, and deacon." These tenets they were called on to abjure, or to suffer suspension from all church benefices. It was also decreed that all the Syrian books on ecclesiastical subjects that could be found, should be burned; "in order," said the inquisitors, "that no pretended apostolical monuments may remain."

The churches on the sea-coast were thus compelled to acknowledge the supremacy of the pope; but they refused to pray in Latin, and insisted on retaining their own language and liturgy. This point they said they would only give up with their lives. The pope compromised with them; Menezes purged their liturgy of its errors; and they retain their Syriac language, and have a Syriac college unto this day. These are called the Syro-Roman churches, and are principally situated on the sea-coast.

The churches in the interior would not yield to Rome. After a show of submission for a little while, they proclaimed eternal war against the inquisition; they hid their books, fled occasionally to the mountains, and sought the protection of the native princes, who had always been proud of their alliance.

Two centuries had elapsed without any particular information concerning the Syrian christians in the interior of India. It was doubted by many whether they existed at all; but if they did exist, it was thought probable that they must possess some interesting documents of christian antiquity. The author conceived the design of visiting them, if practicable, in his tour through Hindostan. He presented a short memoir on the subject in 1805, to Marquis Wellesley, then govenor-general of India; who was pleased to give orders that every facility should be afforded to him in the prosecution of his inquiries. About a year after that nobleman had left India, the author proceeded on his tour. It was necessary that he should visit first the court of the Rajah of Travancore, in whose dominions the Syrian christians resided, that he might obtain permission to pass to their country. The two chief objects which he proposed to himself in exploring the state of this ancient people, were these: First, to investigate their literature and history, and to collect biblical manuscripts. Secondly, if he should find them to be an intelligent people, and well acquainted with the Syriac scriptures, to endeavour to make them instruments of illuminating the southern part of India, by engaging them in translating their scriptures into the native languages. He had reason to believe that this had not yet been done; and he was prepared not to wonder at the delay, by the reflection how long it was before his own countrymen began to think it their duty to make versions of the scriptures, for the use of other nations.

"*Palace of Travancore*, 19*th Oct*, 1806.

"I have now been a week at the palace of Trivanduram, where the Rajah resides. A letter of introduction from Lieut.-Colonel Macaulay, the British resident at Travancore, procured me a proper reception. At my first audience his highness was very inquisitive as to the objects of my journey. As I had servants with me of different casts and languages, it was very easy for the Brahmins to discover every particular they might wish to know, in regard to my profession, pursuits, and manner of life. When I told the Rajah that the Syrian christians were supposed to be of the same religion with the English, he said he thought that could not be the case, else he must have heard it before; if however it was so, he considered my desire to visit them as being very reasonable. I assured his highness that their *Shaster* and ours was the same; and shewed him a Syriac New Testament which I had at hand. The book being bound and gilt after the European manner, the Rajah shook his head, and said he was sure there was not a native in his dominions who could read that book; I observed that this would be proved in a few days. The dewan (or prime minister) thought the character something like what he had seen sometimes in the houses of the *Sooriani*. The Rajah said he would afford me every facility for my journey in his power. He put an emerald ring on my finger, as a mark of his friendship, and to secure me respect in passing through his country; and he directed his dewan to send proper persons with me as guides.

"I requested that the Rajah would be pleased to present a catalogue of all the Hindoo manuscripts in the temples of Travancore to the college of Fort-William in Bengal. The Brahmins were very averse to this; but when I shewed the Rajah the catalogues of the books in the temples of Tanjore, given by the Rajah of Tanjore, and of those of the temple of Ramisseram, given me by order of the Rannie (or queen) of Ramnad, he desired it might be done; and orders have been sent to the Hindoo college of Trichoor for that purpose."*

"*Chinganoor, a Church of the Syrian Christians, Nov. 10th*, 1806.

"From the palace of Travancore I proceeded to Mavely-car, and thence to the hills at the bottom of the high Ghauts which divide the Carnatic from Malayala. The face of the country in general, in the vicinity of the mountains, exhibits a varied scene of hill and dale, and winding streams. These streams fall from the mountains, and preserve the valleys in perpetual verdure. The woods produce pepper, cardamoms, and cassia, or common cinnamon; also frankincense and other aromatic gums. What adds much to the grandeur of the scenery in this country is, that the adjacent mountains of Travancore are not *barren*, but are covered with forests of teak wood; the Indian oak, producing, it is said, the largest timber in the world.

"The first view of the christian churches in this sequestered region of Hindostan, connected with the idea of their tranquil duration for so many ages, cannot fail to excite pleasing emotions in the mind of the beholder. The form of the oldest buildings is not unlike that of some of the old parish churches in England; the style of building in both being of Saracenic origin. They have sloping roofs, pointed arch windows and buttresses supporting the walls. The beams of the roof being exposed to view are ornamented; and the ceiling of the choir and altar is circular and fretted. In the cathedral churches, the shrines of the deceased bishops are placed on each side of the altar. Most of the churches are built of a reddish stone, squared and polished at the quarry; and are of durable construction, the front wall of the largest edifices being six feet thick.

* These three catalogues, together with that of the Rajah of Cochin, which the author procured afterwards, are now deposited in the college of Fort-William, and probably contain all the Hindoo literature of the south of India.

The bells of the churches are cast in the foundries of the country; some of them are of large dimensions, and have inscriptions in Syriac and Malay-alim. In approaching a town in the evening, I once heard the sound of the bells among the hills; a circumstance which made me forget for a moment that I was in Hindostan, and reminded me of *another* country.

"The first Syrian church which I saw was at Mavelycar; but the Syrians here are in the vicinity of the Romish christians; and are not so simple in their manners as those nearer the mountains. They had been often visited by Romish emissaries in former times; and they at first suspected that I belonged to that communion. They had heard of the English, but strangely supposed that they belonged to the church of the pope in the west. They had been so little accustomed to see a friend, that they could not believe that I was come with any friendly purpose. Added to this, I had some discussions with a most intelligent priest, in regard to the original language of the four gospels, which he maintained to be Syriac; and they suspected from the complexion of my argument, that I wished to weaken the evidences for their antiquity.* Soon, however, the gloom and suspicion subsided; they gave me the right

* "You concede," said the Syrian, "that our Saviour spoke in our language; how do you know it?" From Syriac expressions in the Greek gospels. It appears that he spoke Syriac when he walked by the way (Ephphatha), and when he sat in the house (Talitha Cumi), and when he was upon the cross (Eli, Eli, lama sabachthani). The Syrians were pleased when they heard that we had got their language in our English books. The priest observed that these last were not the exact words, but 'Ail, Ail, lamono sabachthani.' I answered that the word must have been very like Eli, for one said 'He calleth Elias.' "True," said he, "but yet it was more likely to be Ail, Ail (pronounced Il or Eel) for Hil or Hila, is old Syriac for vinegar; and one thought he wanted vinegar, and filled immediately a sponge with it. But our Saviour did not want the medicated drink as they supposed.—But, added he, if the parables and discourses of our Lord were in Syriac, and the people of Jerusalem commonly used it, is it not marvellous that his disciples did not record his parables in the Syriac language, and that they should have recourse to the Greek?" I observed that the gospel was for the world, and the Greek was then the universal language, and therefore Providence selected it. "It is very probable," said he, "that the gospels were translated immediately afterwards into Greek, as into other languages; but surely there must have been a Syriac original. The poor people in Jerusalem could not read Greek. Had they no record in their hands of Christ's parables which they had heard, and of his sublime discourses recorded by St. John, after his ascension?" I acknowledged that it was generally believed by the learned that the gospel of St. Matthew was written originally in Syriac. "So you admit St. Matthew? You may as well admit St. John. Or was one gospel enough for the inhabitants of Jerusalem?" I contended that there were many Greek and Roman words in their own Syriac gospels. "True," said he, "Roman words for Roman things." They wished however to see some of these words. The discussion afterwards, particularly in reference to the gospel of St. Luke, was more in my favour.

hand of fellowship, in the primitive manner; and one of their number was deputed to accompany me to the churches in the interior.

"When we were approaching the church of Chinganoor, we met one of the *Cassanars*, or Syrian clergy. He was dressed in a white loose vestment, with a cap of red silk hanging down behind; being informed who he was, I said to him in the Syriac language, 'Peace be unto you.' He was surprised at the salutation; but immediately answered, 'The God of peace be with you.' He accosted the Rajah's servants in the language of the country to know who I was; and immediately returned to the village to announce our approach. When we arrived I was received at the door of the church by three *Kasheeshas*, that is, presbyters, or priests, who were habited in like manner, in white vestments. Their names were Jesu, Zecharias, and Urias, which they wrote down in my journal, each of them adding to his name the title *Kasheesha*. There were also present two *Shumshanas*, or Deacons. The elder priest was a very intelligent man, of reverend appearance, having a long white beard, and of an affable and engaging deportment. The three principal christians, or lay elders belonging to the church were named Abraham, Thoma, and Alexandros. After some conversation with my attendants they received me with confidence and affection; and the people of the neighbouring villages came round, women as well as men. The sight of the WOMEN assured me that I was once more (after a long absence from England) in a christian country. For the Hindoo women, and the Mahomedan women, and in short, all women who are not christians are accounted by the men an inferior race; and, in general, are confined to the house for life, like irrational creatures. In every countenance now before me I thought I could discover the intelligence of christianity. But at the same time, I perceived, all around, symptoms of poverty and political depression. In the churches, and in the people, there was the air of fallen greatness. I said to the senior priest, 'You appear to me like a people who have known better days.' 'It is even so,' said he, 'We are in a degenerate state compared with our forefathers.' He noticed that there were two causes of their present decay. 'About 300 years ago an enemy came from the west bearing the name of Christ, but armed with the inquisition: and compelled us to seek the protection of the native princes. And the native princes have kept us in a state of depression ever since. They indeed recognize our ancient personal privileges, for we rank in general next to the *Nairs*, the nobility of the country; but they have encroached by degrees on our property, till we have been reduced to the humble state in which you find us. The glory of our church has passed away; but we hope your nation will revive it again.' I observed that 'the glory of a church could never die, if it preserved the Bible.' 'We have preserved the Bible,' said he, 'the Hindoo princes never touched our liberty of conscience. We were formerly on a footing with them in political power; and they respect our religion. We have also converts from time to time; but, in this christian duty we are not so active as we once were; besides it is not so creditable now to become christian, in our low estate.' He then pointed out to me a Namboory Brahmin, (that is, a Brahmin of the highest cast) who had lately become a christian and assumed the white vestment of a Syrian priest. 'The learning too of the Bible,' he added, 'is in a low state amongst us. Our copies are few in number; and that number is diminishing instead of increasing; and the writing out a whole copy of the sacred scriptures is a great labour, where there is no profit and little piety.' I then produced a printed copy of the Syriac New Testament. There was not one of them who had ever seen a printed copy before. They admired it much; and every priest, as it came into his hands, began to read a portion, which he did fluently, while the women came round to hear. I asked the old priest whether I should send them some copies from Europe. 'They would be worth their weight in silver,' said he. He asked me whether the Old Testament was printed in Syriac, as well as the New. I told him it was, but I had not a copy. They professed an earnest desire to obtain some copies of the *whole* Syriac Bible; and asked whether it would be practicable to obtain one copy for every church. 'I must confess to you,' said Zecharias, 'that we have very few copies of the *prophetical* scriptures in the church. Our church languishes for want of the scriptures.' But he added, 'the language that is most in use among the people, is the Malayalim, (or Malabar) the vernacular language of the country. The Syriac is now only the learned language, and the language of the church; but we generally expound the scriptures to the people in the vernacular tongue.'

"I then entered on the subject of the translation of the scriptures. He said, 'a version could be made with critical accuracy; for there were many of the Syrian clergy who were perfect masters of both languages, having spoken them from their infancy. But,' said he, 'our bishop will rejoice to see you, and to discourse with you on this and other subjects.' I told them that if a translation could be prepared, I should be able to get it printed, and to distribute copies among their fifty-five churches at a small price. 'That indeed would give joy,' said old Abraham. There was here a murmur of satisfaction among the people. If I understand you right, said I, the greatest blessing the English church can bestow upon you, is the Bible. 'It is so,' said he. 'And what is the next greatest,' said I. 'Some freedom and personal consequence as a people.' By which he meant political liberty. 'We are here in bondage, like Israel in Egypt.' I observed that the English nation would doubtless recognize a nation of fellow-christians; and would be happy to interest itself in their behalf, as far as our political relation with the prince of the country would permit. They wished to know what were the principles of the English government, civil and religious. I answered that our government might be said to be founded generally on the principles of the Bible. 'Ah,' said old Zecharias, 'that must be a glorious government which is founded on the principles of the Bible.' The priests then desired I would give them some account of the history of the English nation, and of our secession from their enemy, the church of Rome. And in return, I requested they would give me some account of their history. My communications with the Syrians are rendered very easy, by means of an interpreter whom I brought with me all the way from the Tanjore country. He is a Hindoo by descent, but is an intelligent christian, and was a pupil and catechist of the late Mr. Swartz. The Rev. Mr. Kohloff recommended him to me. He formerly lived in Travancore, and is well acquainted with the vernacular tongue. He also reads and writes English very well, and is as much interested in favour of the Syrian christians as I myself. Besides Mr. Swartz's catechist, there are two natives of Travancore here, who speak the Hindostanee language, which is familiar to me. My knowledge of the Syriac is sufficient to refer to texts of scriptures; but I do not well understand the pronunciation of the Syrians. I hope to be better acquainted with their language before I leave the country."

"*Ranniel, a Syrian Church, Nov. 12th,* 1806.

"This church is built upon a rocky hill on the banks of the river; and is the most remote of all the churches in this quarter. The two *Kusheeshas* here are Lucas and Mattai (Luke and Matthew). The chief lay members are Abraham, Georgius, Thoma, and Philippus. Some of the priests accompany me from church to church. I have now visited eight churches, and scarcely believe sometimes that I am in the land of the Hindoos; only that I now and then see a Hindoo temple on the banks of the river. I observed that the bells of most of the churches are within the building, and not in a tower. The reason they said was this: when a Hindoo temple happens to be near a church, the Hindoos do not like the bell to sound loud, for they say it frightens their god.—I perceive that the Syrian christians assimilate much to the Hindoos in the practice of frequent ablutions for health and cleanliness, and in the use of vegetables and light food.

"I attended divine service on the Sunday. Their liturgy is that which was formerly used in the churches of the patriarch of Antioch. During the prayers, there were intervals of silence; the priest praying in a low voice, and every man praying for himself. These silent intervals add much to the solemnity and appearance of devotion. They use incense in the churches, it grows in the woods around them; and contributes much, they say, to health, and to the warmth and comfort of the church, during the cold and rainy season of the year.—At the conclusion of the service, a ceremony takes place which pleased me much. The priest (or bishop, if he be present) comes forward, and all the people pass by him as they go out, receiving his benediction individually. If any man has been guilty of any immorality, he does not receive the blessing; and this, in their primitive and patriarchal state, is accounted a severe punishment.—Instruction by preaching is little in use among them now. Many of the old men lamented the decay of piety, and religious knowledge; and spoke with pleasure of the record of ancient times.—They have some ceremonies nearly allied to those of the Greek church. Here, as in all churches in a state of decline, there is too much formality in the worship. But they have the Bible and a scriptural liturgy; and these will save a church in the worst of times. These may preserve the spark and life of religion, though the flame be out. And as there were but few copies of the Bible among the Syrians (for every copy was transcribed with the pen) it is highly probable that, if they had not enjoyed the advantage of the daily prayers, and daily portions of scripture in their liturgy there would have been in the revolution of ages, no vestige of christianity left among them.*

"The doctrines of the Syrian christians are few in number, but pure, and agree in essential points with those of the church of England; so that, although the body of the church appears to be ignorant, and formal, and dead, there are individuals who are alive to righteousness, who are distinguished from the rest by their purity of life, and are sometimes censured for too rigid a piety.—In every church, and in many of the private houses, there are manuscripts in the Syriac language; and I have been successful in procuring some old and

* In a nation like ours overflowing with knowledge, men are not always in circumstances to perceive the value of a scriptural liturgy. When christians are well taught, they think they want something better. But the young and the ignorant, who form a great proportion of the community, are edified by a little plain instruction frequently repeated. A small church or sect may do without a form for a while; but a national liturgy is that which preserves a relic of the true faith among the people in a large empire, when the priests leave their ARTICLES and their CONFESSIONS of FAITH. Woe to the declining church which hath no gospel liturgy! Witness the Presbyterians in the West of England, and some other sects, who are said to have become Arians and Socinians to a man. The Puritans of a former age did not live long enough to see the use of an evangelical formulary.

valuable copies of the scriptures and other books, written in different ages and in different characters."

"*Cande-nad, a Church of the Syrian Christians, November* 23, 1806.

"This is the residence of Mar Dionysius, the Metropolitan of the Syrian church. A great number of the priests from the other churches had assembled, by desire of the bishop, before my arrival. The bishop resides in a building attached to the church. I was much struck with his first appearance. He was dressed in a vestment of dark red silk; a large golden cross hung from his neck, and his venerable beard reached below his girdle. Such, thought I, was the appearance of Chrysostom in the fourth century. On public occasions, he wears the episcopal mitre, and a muslin robe is thrown over his under garment; and in his hand he bears the crosier, or pastoral staff.—He is a man of highly respectable character in his church, eminent for his piety, and for the attention he devotes to his sacred functions. I found him to be far superior in general learning to any of his clergy whom I had yet seen. He told me that all my conversations with his priests since my arrival in the country had been communicated to him. 'You have come,' said he, 'to visit a declining church, and I am now an old man; but the hopes of its seeing better days cheer my old age, though I may not live to see them.'—I submitted to the bishop my wishes in regard to the translation and printing of the holy scriptures. 'I have already fully considered the subject,' said he, 'and have determined to superintend the work myself, and to call the most learned of my clergy to my aid. It is a work which will illuminate these dark regions, and God will give it his blessing.' I was much pleased when I heard this pious resolution of the venerable man; for I had now ascertained that there were upwards of 200,000 christians in the south of India, besides the Syrians who speak the Malabar language.—The next subject of importance in my mind, was the collection of useful manuscripts in the Chaldaic and Syriac languages; and the bishop was pleased to say that he would assist my inquiries and add to my collection.—He descanted with great satisfaction on the hope of seeing printed Syriac Bibles from England; and said they would be 'a treasure to his church.'"

"*Cande-nad, 24th November*, 1806.

"Since my coming amongst this people, I had cherished the hope that they might be one day united with the church of England. When I reflected on the immense power of the Romish church in India, and on our inability to withstand its influence, alone, it appeared to be an object of great consequence to secure the aid and co-operation of the Syrian church, and the sanction of its antiquity in the east. I thought it might be serviceable, at least, to lay such a foundation by the discussion of the subject, as our church might act upon hereafter, if she should think it expedient. I was afraid to mention the subject to the bishop at our first interview; but he himself intimated that he would be glad if I would communicate freely upon it with two of his clergy.—I had hitherto observed somewhat of a reserve in those with whom I had conversed on this matter; and now the cause was explained. The bishop's chaplains confessed to me that they had doubts as to the purity of English ordination. 'The English,' said they, 'may be a warlike and great people; but their church, by your own account, is but of recent origin. Whence do you derive your ordination?' From Rome. 'You derive it from a church which is our ancient enemy, and with which we would never unite.'—They acknowledged that there might be salvation in every church where 'the name of Christ was named;' but in the question of an UNION, it was to be considered that they had existed a pure church of Christ from the earliest ages; that if there was such a thing in the world as ordination by the laying on of hands, in succession from the Apostles, it was probable that they possessed it; that there was no record of history or tradition to impeach their claim. I observed that there was reason to believe that the same ordination had descended from the Apostles to the church of Rome. 'It might be so; but that church had departed from the faith.' I answered that the impurity of the channel had not corrupted the ordinance itself, or invalidated the legitimacy of the imposition of hands; any more than the wickedness of a high priest in Israel could disqualify his successors. The church of England assumed that she derived apostolical ordination *through* the church of Rome, as she might have derived it *through* the church of Antioch. I did not consider that the church of England was entitled to reckon her ordination to be higher or more sacred than that of the Syrian church. This was the point upon which they wished me to be explicit. They expected that in any official negociation on this subject, the antiquity and purity of Syrian ordination should be expressly admitted.

"Our conversation was reported to the bishop. He wished me to state the advantages of an union. One advantage would be, I observed, that English clergymen, or rather missionaries ordained by the church of England, might be permitted hereafter to preach in the numerous churches of the Syrians in India, and aid them in the promulgation of pure religion, against the preponderating and increasing influence of the Romish church. And again, That ordination by the Syrian bishop might qualify for preaching in the English churches in India; for we had an immense empire in Hindostan, but few preachers; and of these few scarcely any could preach in the native languages.—The bishop said 'I would sacrifice much for such an union; only let me not be called to compromise any thing of the dignity and purity of our church.' I told him, we did not wish to degrade, we would rather protect and defend it. All must confess that it was Christ's church in the midst of a heathen land. The church of England would be happy to promote its welfare, to revive its spirit, and to use it as an instrument of future good in the midst of her own empire. I took this occasion to observe that there were some rites and practices in the Syrian church, which our church might consider objectionable or nugatory. The bishop confessed that some customs had been introduced during their decline in the latter centuries, which had no necessary connection with the constitution of the church, and might be removed without inconvenience. He asked whether I had authority from my own church to make any proposition to him. I answered that I had not; that my own church scarcely knew that the Syrian church existed; but I could anticipate the wishes and purposes of good men. He thought it strange that there was no bishop in India to superintend so large an empire; and said he did not perfectly comprehend our ecclesiastical principles. I told him that we had sent bishops to other countries; but that our Indian empire was yet in its infancy.—Next day, the bishop, after conferring with his clergy on the subject, returned an answer in writing to the following effect; 'That an union with the English church, or, at least, such a connection as should appear to both churches practicable and expedient, would be a happy event and favourable to the advancement of religion in India.' In making this communication, he used his official designation, 'Mar Dionysius, Metropolitan of Malabar.'—I asked the bishop if he would permit two of the young Cassanars to go to England to finish their education, and then return to India. He said he should be very happy to give his permission, if any should be found who were willing to go. I have accordingly made the offer to two youths of good abilities, who are well skilled in the Syriac language."

"*Cande-nad,* 25*th Nov.*

"The bishop was desirous to know something of the other churches which had separated from Rome. I was ashamed to tell him how many they were. I mentioned that there was a *Kasheesha* or Presbyter church in our own kingdom, in which every Kasheesha was equal to another. 'And are there no *Shimshanas?*' (Deacons in holy orders). None. 'And what, is there nobody to overlook the Kasheeshas?' Not one. 'There must be something imperfect there,' said he.* This led to

* It is proper to state for the satisfaction of those who may differ in opinion with the venerable bishop, that in the Syriac translation of the New Testament, there is no proper word for bishop other than Kasheesha. The words Kasheesha and Shumshana, or properly Me-shumshana, are the two terms for the two

the mention of the different sects. Those which most interested him were the Quakers and Baptists. He said it was an imposing idea to wash the body with water, to begin a new life. He asked whether they were baptized again every time they relapsed into sin and known apostacy.—'Are there good men amongst these sects?' Excellent men almost in all. 'I see it is with you as it was in the first ages, new sects were produced by true piety, but it was piety founded on ignorance. But do not good men in these sects relax a little when they grow old?'—Yes, they speak in general less frequently and less dogmatically of their peculiar forms when they are old; one reason of which is, that the smaller sects, who are, for the most part, poor, generally acquire their competence of learning in advanced life.—We next had some conversation concerning forms of worship; whether Christ intended that his church should have the same form under the burning line, and in a country of frost and snow."

"*Udiamper, Dec.* 1806.

"From Cande-nad I returned to the sea-coast to visit Lieut.-Colonel Macaulay, the British resident in Travancore. He is at present on the island of Bal-gatty, called by the natives the Pepper Jungle. I have derived much valuable information from this intelligent officer, who possesses a better knowledge of the south of India, than, I suppose, any other European. He is a gentleman of a highly cultivated mind, of much various learning, and master of several languages. To these attainments he adds a quality which does not always accompany them.—He is the friend of christianity. After residing with him a few days, he accompanied me in a tour to the interior. We first visited Udiamper, or as it is called by the Portuguese writers, Diamper. This was formerly the residence of Beliarte, king of the

orders of bishop and deacon in the third chapter of 1st Timothy. The terms Episcopos and Methropolita have been introduced into the Syrian church from the Greek. The bishop seemed to be more surprised at the striking out the sacred order of deacon, than at the not finding the order of a superintending priest or bishop.

Christians; and here is the Syrian church at which Archbishop Menezes from Goa, convened the synod of the Syrian clergy in 1599, when he burned the Syriac and Chaldaic books. The Syrians report, that while the flames ascended, he went round the church in procession, chaunting a song of triumph.

"From Udiamper, Colonel Macaulay accompanied me to Cande-nad, to visit the Syrian bishop a second time. He told us he had commenced the translation of the scriptures. He was rather indisposed, and said he felt the infirmities of advanced years, his age being now seventy-eight. I promised to see him once more before I left the country."

"*Cranganore, 9th Dec.* 1806.

"This is that celebrated place of christian antiquity where the apostle Thomas is said to have landed, when he first arrived in India from Aden in Arabia. There was formerly a town and fort at Cranganore, the Portuguese having once thought of making it the emporium of their commerce in India; but both are now in ruins. There is however one substantial relic of its greatness. There is an archbishop of Cranganore, and subject to him there are forty-five churches; many of which I entered. In some of them the worship is conducted with as much decorum as in the Romish churches of Western Ireland. Not far from Cranganore is the town of PAROOR, where there is an ancient Syrian church, which bears the name of the Apostle Thomas. It is supposed to be the oldest in Malabar, and is still used for divine service. I took a drawing of it. The tradition among the Syrians is, that the apostle continued at this place for a time, before he went to preach at Melapoor and St. Thomas's Mount, on the coast of Coromandel, where he was put to death.—The fact is certainly of little consequence; but I am satisfied that we have as good authority for believing that the apostle Thomas died in India, as that the apostle Peter died at Rome."

"*Verapoli, Dec.* 1806.

"This is the residence of bishop Raymondo, the pope's apostolic vicar in Malabar. There is a college here for the sacerdotal office, in which the students (from ten to twenty in number) are instructed in the *Latin* and *Syriac* languages.—At Pulingunna there is another college, in which the Syriac alone is taught. Here I counted twelve students. The apostolic vicar superintends sixty-four churches; exclusive of the forty-five governed by the archbishop of Cranganore, and exclusive of the large dioceses of the bishops of Cochin and of Quilon, whose churches extend to Cape Comorin, and are visible from the sea. The view of this assemblage of christian congregations excited in my mind mingled sensations of pleasure and regret; of pleasure to think that so many of the Hindoos had been rescued from the idolatry of Brahma, and its criminal worship; and of regret when I reflected that there was not to be found among the whole body, one copy of the Holy Bible.

"The apostolic vicar is an Italian, and corresponds with the society 'de propaganda Fide.' He is a man of liberal manners, and gave me free access to the archives of Verapoli, which are upwards of two centuries old. In the library I found many volumes marked 'Liber heriticus prohibitus.' Every step I take in christian India, I meet with a memento of the inquisition. The apostolical vicar, however, does not acknowledge its authority, and places himself under British protection. He spoke of the inquisition with just indignation, and in the presence of the British resident, called it 'a horrid tribunal.' I asked him whether he thought I might with safety visit the inquisition, when I sailed past Goa; there being at this time a British force in its vicinity. It asserted a personal jurisdiction over natives who were now British subjects; and it was proper the English Government should know something of its present state. The bishop answered, 'I do not know what you might do, under the protection of a British force; but I should not like (smiling, and pressing his capacious sides,) to trust *my* body in their hands.'

"We then had some conversation on the subject of

giving the scriptures to the native Roman Catholics. I had heard before, that the bishop was by no means hostile to the measure. I told him that I should probably find the means of translating the scriptures into the Malabar language, and wished to know whether he had any objection to this mode of illuminating the ignorant minds of the native christians. He said he had none. I visited the bishop two or three times afterwards. At our last interview he said, 'I have been thinking of the good gift you are meditating for the native christians; but believe me, the inquisition will endeavour to counteract your purposes by every means in their power. I afterwards conversed with an intelligent native priest, who was well acquainted with the state and character of the christians, and asked him whether he thought they would be happy to obtain the scriptures?—'Yes,' answered he, '*those who have heard of them.*' I asked if he had got a Bible himself?—'No,' he said, 'but he had seen one at Goa.'"

"*Angamalee, a Syrian town, containing three churches, January*, 1807.

"I have penetrated once more inland, to visit the Syrian churches. At the town of Cenotta, I was surprised to meet with Jews and christians in the same street. The Jews led me first to their synagogue, and allowed me to take away some manuscripts for money. The Syrian christians then conducted me to their ancient church. I afterwards sat down on an emmence above the town, to contemplate this interesting spectacle; a Jewish synagogue, and a christian church, standing over against each other; exhibiting, as it were, during many revolving ages, the LAW and the GOSPEL to the view of the heathen people.

"Angamalee is one of the most remote of the Syrian towns in this direction, and is situated on a high land. This was once the residence of the Syrian bishop. The inhabitants told me, that when *Tippoo* Sultan invaded Travancore, a detachment of his cavalry penetrated to Angamalee, where they expected to find great wealth, from its ancient fame. Being Mahomedans, they expressed their abhorrence of the christian religion, by destroying one of the lesser churches, and stabling their horses in the great church.—In this place I have found a good many valuable manuscripts. I had been led to suppose, from the statement of the Portuguese historians, that possibly all the Syriac MSS. of the Bible had been burned by the Romish church at the synod of Diamper, in 1599. But this was not the case; the inquisitors condemned many books to the flames; but they saved the Bible; being content to order that the Syriac scriptures should be amended agreeably to the vulgate of Rome. But many Bibles and other volumes were not produced at all. In the acts of the Council of Nice it is recorded, that Johannes bishop of India signed his name at that Council in A. D. 325. The Syriac version of the scriptures was brought to India, according to the popular belief, before the year 325. Some of their present copies are certainly of ancient date. Though written on a strong thick paper, like that of some MSS. in the British Museum, commonly called eastern paper, the ink has, in several places, eat through the material in the exact form of the letter. In other copies, where the ink had less of a corroding quality, it has fallen off, and left a dark vestige of the letter, faint indeed, but not, in general, illegible. There is a volume, which was deposited in one of the remote churches, near the mountains, which merits a particular description; it contains the Old and New Testaments, engrossed on strong vellum, in large folio, having three columns in a page; and is written with beautiful accuracy. The character is Estrangelo Syriac; and the words of every book are numbered. But the volume has suffered injury from time or neglect. In certain places the ink has been totally obliterated from the page, and left the parchment in its state of natural whiteness; but the letters can, in general, be distinctly traced from the impress of the pen, or from the partial corrosion of the ink.—I scarcely expected that the Syrian church would have parted with this manuscript. But the bishop was pleased to present it to me, saying, 'It will be safer in your hands than in our own;' alluding to the revolutions in Hindostan.—'And yet,' said he, 'we have kept it, as some think, for near a thousand years.'—

'I wish,' said I, 'that England may be able to keep it a thousand years.'—In looking over it, I find the very first proposed emendation of the Hebrew text by Dr. Kennicott (Gen. iv. 8.) in this manuscript; and, no doubt, it is the right reading. The disputed passage in 1 John v. 7. is not to be found in it; nor is this verse to be found in any copy of the Syriac scriptures which I have yet seen. But notwithstanding this omission, and notwithstanding the great display of learning in maintaining a contrary opinion, I believe the passage to be genuine. The view of these copies of the scriptures, and of the churches which contain them, still continues to excite a pleasing astonishment in my mind; and I sometimes question myself, whether I am indeed in India, in the midst of the Hindoos, and not far from the equinoctial line. How wonderful it is, that, during the dark ages of Europe, whilst ignorance and superstition, in a manner, denied the scriptures to the rest of the world, the Bible should have found an asylum in the mountains of Malay-ala; where it was freely read by upwards of an hundred churches!

"But there are other ancient documents in Malabar, not less interesting than the Syrian manuscripts. The old Portuguese historians relate, that soon after the arrival of their countrymen in India, about 300 years ago, the Syrian bishop of Angamalee (the place where I now am) deposited in the Fort of Cochin, for safe custody, certain *tablets of brass*, on which were engraved rights of nobility, and other privileges granted by a prince of a former age; and that while these tablets were under the charge of the Portuguese, they had been unaccountably lost, and were never after heard of. Adrian Moens, a governor of Cochin in 1770, who published some account of the Jews of Malabar, informs us that he used every means in his power, for many years, to obtain a sight of the famed christian plates; and was at length satisfied that they were irrecoverably lost, or rather, he adds, that *they never existed*. The learned in general, and the antiquarian in particular, will be glad to hear that these ancient tablets have been recovered within this last month by the exertions of Lieut.-Colonel Macaulay, the British resident in Travancore, and are now officially deposited with that officer.

"The christian tablets are six in number. They are composed of a mixed metal. The engraving on the largest plate is thirteen inches long, by about four broad. They are closely written, four of them on both sides of the plate, making in all eleven pages. On the plate reputed to be the oldest, there is writing perspicuously engraved in *nail-headed* or triangular-headed letters, resembling the *Persepolitan* or Babylonish. On the same plate there is writing in another character, which is supposed to have no affinity with any existing character in Hindostan. The grant on this plate appears to be witnessed by four Jews of rank, whose names are distinctly engraved in an old Hebrew character, resembling the alphabet called the *Palmyrene*; and to each name is prefixed the title of '*Magen*,' or chief, as the Jews translated it.—It may be doubted, whether there exist in the world many documents of so great length, which are of equal antiquity, and in such faultless preservation, as the christian tablets of Malabar. The Jews of Cochin indeed contest the palm of antiquity, for they also produce two tablets, containing privileges granted at a remote period; of which they presented to me a Hebrew translation. As no person can be found in this country who is able to translate the christian tablets, I have directed an engraver at Cochin to execute a copper-plate fac-simile of the whole, for the purpose of transmitting copies to the learned societies in Asia and Europe. The Christian and Jewish plates together make fourteen pages. A copy was sent in the first instance to the pundits of the Sanscrit college at Trichiur, by direction of the Rajah of Cochin; but they could not read the character.*—From this place I proceed to Cande-nad, to visit the bishop once more before I return to Bengal."

THE MALABAR BIBLE.

After the author left Travancore, the bishop prosecuted the translation of the scriptures into the Malabar

* Most of the manuscripts which I collected among the Syrian christians, I have presented to the University of Cambridge; and they are now deposited in the public library of that university, together with the copper-plate fac-similes of the Christian and Jewish tablets.

language without intermission, until he had completed the New Testament. The year following, the author visited Travancore a second time, and carried the manuscript to Bombay to be printed! an excellent fount of Malabar types having been recently cast at that place. Learned natives went from Travancore to superintend the press; and it is probable that it is now nearly finished, as a copy of the gospels of St. Matthew and St. Mark, beautifully printed, was received in England some time ago. This version of the scriptures will be prosecuted until the whole Bible is completed, and copies circulated throughout the christian regions of Malabar.

THE SYRIAC BIBLE.

It has been further in contemplation to print an edition of the Syriac scriptures, if the public should countenance the design. This gift, it may be presumed, the English nation will be pleased to present to the Syrian christians. We are already debtors to that ancient people. They have preserved the manuscripts of the holy scriptures incorrupt, during a long series of ages, and have now committed them into our own hands. By their long and energetic defence of pure doctrine against anti-christian error, they are entitled to the gratitude and thanks of the rest of the christian world. Further, they have preserved to this day the language in which our blessed Lord preached to men the glad tidings of salvation. Their scriptures, their doctrine, their language, in short their very existence, all add something to the evidence of the truth of christianity.

The motives then for printing an edition of the Syriac Bible are these:—

1. To do honour to the language which was spoken by our blessed Saviour when upon earth.

2. To do honour to that ancient church, which has preserved his language and his doctrine.

3. As the means of perpetuating the true faith in the same church for ages to come.

4. As the means of preserving the pronunciation, and of cultivating the knowledge of the Syriac language in the east; and

5. As the means of reviving the knowledge of the Syriac language in our own nation.

On the author's return to England, he could not find one copy of the Syriac Bible in a separate volume for sale in the kingdom. He wished to send a copy to the Syrian bishop, as an earnest of more, when an edition should be printed.

The Syriac Bible is wanted not only by the churches of the Syrian christians, but by the still more numerous churches of the Syro-Romish christians in Malabar, who also use the Syriac language.

THE ROMISH CHRISTIANS IN INDIA.

In every age of the church of Rome there have been individuals, of an enlightened piety, who derived their religion not from "the commandments of men," but from the doctrines of the Bible. There are, at this day, in India and in England, members of that communion, who deserve the affection and respect of all good men; and whose cultivated minds will arraign the corruptions of their own religion, which the author is about to describe, more severely than he will permit himself to do. He is indeed prepared to speak of Roman catholics with as much liberality as perhaps any protestant has ever attempted on christian principles; for he is aquainted with individuals, whose unaffected piety he considers a reproach to a great body of protestants, even of the strictest sort. It is indeed painful to say any thing which may seem to feeling and noble minds ungenerous; but those enlightened persons, whose good opinion it is desirable to preserve, will themselves be pleased to see that truth is not sacrificed to personal respect, or to a spurious candour. Their own church sets an example of "plainness of speech" in the assertion of those tenets which it professes, some of which must be extremely painful to the feeling of protestants, in their social intercourse with catholics; such as "That there is no salvation out of the pale of the Romish church."

This exclusive character prevents concord and intimacy between protestant and catholic families. On the principles of infidelity they can associate very easily; but on the principles of religion, the protestant must ever be on the *defensive;* for the Romish church excommunicates him; and although he must hope that some individuals do not maintain the tenet, yet his uncertainty as to the fact prevents that cordiality which he desires. Many excellent catholics suffer unjustly in their intercourse with protestants, from the ancient and exclusive articles of their own church, which they themselves neither profess nor believe. If they will only intimate to their protestant friends, that they renounce the exclusive principle, and that they profess the religion of the Bible, no more seems requisite to form with such persons the sincerest friendship on christian principles.

At the present time we see the Romish religion in Europe *without* dominion; and hence it is viewed by the mere philosopher with indifference or contempt. He is pleased to see, that the "seven heads and the ten horns" are taken away; and thinks nothing of the "names of blasphemy." But in the following pages, the author will have occasion to shew what Rome is, as *having* dominion; and possessing it too within the boundaries of the British empire.

In passing through the Romish provinces in the east, though the author had before heard much of the papal corruptions, he certainly did not expect to see christianity in the degraded state in which he found it. Of the priests it may truly be said, that they are, in general, better acquainted with the Veda of Brahma than with the gospel of Christ. In some places the doctrines of both are blended. At Aughoor, situated between Tritchinopoly and Madura, he witnessed (in October 1806) the tower of Juggernaut employed to solemnize a christian festival. The old priest Josephus accompanied him, when he surveyed the idolatrous car and its painted figures, and gave him a particular account of the various ceremonies which are performed, seemingly unconscious himself of any impropriety in them. The author went with him afterwards into the church, and seeing a book lying on the altar, opened it; but the reader may judge of his surprise, when he found it was a Syriac volume, and was informed that the priest himself was a descendant of the Syrian christians, and belonged to what is now called the Syro-Roman church, the whole service of which is in Syriac.—Thus, by the intervention of the Papal power, are the ceremonies of Moloch consecrated in a manner by the sacred Syriac language. What a heavy responsibility lies on Rome, for having thus corrupted and degraded that pure and ancient church!

While the author viewed these christian corruptions in different places, and in different forms, he was always referred to the inquisition at Goa, as the fountain-head. He had long cherished the hope, that he should be able to visit Goa before he left India. His chief objects were the following:—

1. To ascertain whether the inquisition actually refused to recognise the Bible, among the Romish churches in British India.

2. To inquire into the state and jurisdiction of the inquisition, particularly as it affected British subjects.

3. To learn what was the system of education for the priesthood; and

4. To examine the ancient church libraries in Goa, which were said to contain all the books of the first printing.

He will select from his journal, in this place, chiefly what relates to the inquisition. He had learnt from every quarter, that this tribunal, formerly so well known for its frequent burnings, was still in operation, though under some restriction as to the *publicity* of its proceedings; and that its power extended to the extreme boundary of Hidostan. That, in the present civilized state of christian nations in Europe, an inquisition should exist at all under their authority, appeared strange; but that a Papal tribunal of this character should exist under the implied toleration and countenance of the British government; that christians, being subjects of the British empire, and inhabiting the British territories, should be amenable to its power and jurisdiction, was a statement which seemed to be scarcely credible; but, if true, a fact which demanded the most public and solemn representation.

"*Goa, Convent of the Augustinians,*
Jan. 23, 1808.

"On my arrival at Goa, I was received into the house of Captain Schuyler, the British resident. The British force here is commanded by Colonel Adams, of his majesty's 78th regiment, with whom I was formerly well acquainted in Bengal.* Next day I was introduced by these gentlemen to the vice-roy of Goa, the Count de Cabral. I intimated to his excellency my wish to sail up the river to Old Goa,† (where the inquisition is,) to which he politely acceded. Major Pareira, of the Portuguese establishment, who was present, and to whom I had letters of introduction from Bengal, offered to accompany me to the city, and to introduce me to the archbishop of Goa, the primate of the Orient.

"I had communicated to Colonel Adams, and to the British resident, my purpose of inquiring into the state of the inquisition. These gentlemen informed me, that I should not be able to accomplish my design without difficulty; since every thing relating to the inquisition was conducted in a very secret manner, the most respectable of the lay Portuguese themselves being ignorant of its proceedings; and that, if the priests were to discover my object, their excessive jealousy and alarm would prevent their communicating with me, or satisfying my inquiries on any subject.

"On receiving this intelligence, I perceived that it would be necessary to proceed with caution. I was, in fact, about to visit a republic of priests; whose dominion had existed for nearly three centuries; whose province it was to prosecute heretics, and particularly the teachers of heresy; and from whose authority and sentence there was no appeal in India.‡

* The forts in the harbour of Goa were then occupied by British troops (two king's regiments, and two regiments of native infantry) to prevent its falling into the hands of the French.

† There is Old and New Goa. The old city is about eight miles up the river. The vice-roy and the chief Portuguese inhabitants reside at New Goa, which is at the mouth of the river, within the forts of the harbour. The old city, where the inquisition and the churches are, is now almost entirely deserted by the secular Portuguese, and is inhabited by the priests alone. The unhealthiness of the place, and the ascendency of the priests, are the causes assigned for abandoning the ancient city.

‡ I was informed that the vice-roy of Goa has no authority over the inquisition, and that he himself is liable to its censure. Were the British government, for instance, to prefer a complaint against the inquisition to the Portuguese

"It happened that Lieutenant Kempthorne, Commander of his majesty's birg Diana, a distant connection of my own, was at this time in the harbour. On his learning that I meant to visit Old Goa, he offered to accompany me; as did Captain Stirling, of his majesty's 84th regiment, which is now stationed at the forts.

"We proceeded up the river in the British resident's barge, accompanied by Major Pareira, who was well qualified, by a thirty years' residence, to give information concerning local circumstances. From him I learned that there were upwards of two hundred churches and chapels in the province of Goa, and upwards of two thousand priests.

"On our arrival at the city,* it was past twelve o'clock; all the churches were shut, and we were told that they would not be opened again till two o'clock. I mentioned to Major Pareira, that I intended to stay at Old Goa some days; and that I should be obliged to him to find me a place to sleep in. He seemed surprised at this intimation, and observed that it would be difficult for me to obtain a reception in any of the churches or convents, and that there were no private houses into which I could be admitted. I said I could sleep anywhere; I had two servants with me and a travelling bed. When he perceived that I was serious in my purpose, he gave directions to a civil officer, in that place, to clear out a room in a building which had been long uninhabited, and which was then used as a warehouse for goods. Matters at this time presented a very gloomy appearance; and I had thoughts of returning with my companions from this inhospitable place. In the mean time we sat down in the room I have just mentioned, to take some refreshment, while Major Pareira went to call on some of his friends. During this interval, I communicated to Lieutenant Kempthorne the object of my

government at Goa, it could obtain no redress. By the very constitution of the inquisition, there is no power in India which can invade its jurisdiction, or even put a question to it on any subject.

* We entered the city by the palace gate, over which is the statue of Vasco de Gama, who first opened India to the view of Europe. I had seen at Calicut, a few weeks before, the ruins of the SAMORIN's palace, in which Vasco de Gama was first received. The Samorin was the first native prince against whom the Europeans made war. The empire of the Samorin has passed away; and the empire of his conquerors has passed away; and now imperial Britain exercises dominion. May imperial Britain be prepared to give a good account of her stewardship, when it shall be said unto her, "Thou mayest be no longer steward!"

visit. I had in my pocket 'Dellon's account of the Inquisition at Goa;'* and I mentioned some particulars. While we were conversing on the subject, the great bell of the cathedral began to toll; the same which Dellon observes always tolls, before day-light, on the morning of the Auto da Fe. I did not myself ask any questions of the people concerning the inquisition; but Mr. Kempthorne made inquiries for me; and he soon found out that the Santa Casa, or holy office, was close to the house where we were then sitting. The gentlemen went to the window to view the horrid mansion; and I could see the indignation of free and enlightened men arise in the countenances of the two British officers, while they contemplated a place where formerly their own countrymen were condemned to the flames, and into which they themselves might now suddenly be thrown, without the possibility of rescue.

"At two o'clock we went out to view the churches, which were now open for the afternoon service; for there are regular daily masses; and the bells began to assail the ear in every quarter.

"The magnificence of the churches of Goa far exceeded any idea I had formed from the previous description. Goa is properly a city of churches; and the wealth of provinces seems to have been expended in their erection. The ancient specimens of architecture at this place far excel any thing that has been attempted in modern times in any other part of the east, both in grandeur and in taste. The chapel of the palace is built after the plan of St. Peter's at Rome, and is said to be an accurate model of that paragon of architecture. The church of St. Dominic, the founder of the inquisition, is decorated with paintings of Italian masters. St. Francis Xavier lies enshrined in a monument of exquisite art, and his coffin is enchased with silver and *precious stones*. The cathedral of Goa is worthy of one of the principal cities of Europe; and the church and convent of the Augustinians (in which I now reside) is a noble pile of building, situated on an eminence, and has a magnificent appearance from afar.

* Monsieur Dellon, a physician, was imprisoned in the dungeon of the inquisition at Goa for two years, and witnessed an Auto da Fe, when some heretics were burned; at which he walked barefoot. After his release he wrote the history of his confinement. His descriptions are in general very accurate.

"But what a contrast to all this grandeur of the churches is the worship offered in them! I have been present at the service in one or other of the chapels every day since I arrived; and I seldom see a single worshipper, but the ecclesiastics. Two rows of native priests, kneeling in order before the altar, clothed in coarse black garments, of sickly appearance and vacant countenance, perform here, from day to day, their laborious masses, seemingly unconscious of any other duty or obligation of life.

"The day was now far spent, and my companions were about to leave me. While I was considering whether I should return with them, Major Pareira said he would first introduce me to a priest, high in office, and one of the most learned men in the place. We accordingly walked to the convent of the Augustinians, where I was presented to Josephus a Doloribus, a man well advanced in life, of pale visage and penetrating eye, rather of a reverend appearance, and possessing great fluency of speech and urbanity of manners. At first sight he presented the aspect of one of those acute and prudent men of the world, the learned and respectable Italian Jesuits, some of whom are yet found, since the demolition of their order, reposing in tranquil obscurity, in different parts of the east. After half an hour's conversation in the Latin language, during which he adverted rapidly to a variety of subjects, and inquired concerning some learned men of his own church, whom I had visited in my tour, he politely invited me to take up my residence with him, during my stay at Old Goa. I was highly gratified by this unexpected invitation; but Lieutenant Kempthorne did not approve of leaving me in the hands of the *inquisitor*. For judge of our surprise, when we discovered that my learned host was one of the inquisitors of the holy office, the second member of that august tribunal in rank, but the first and most active agent in the business of the department. Apartments were assigned to me in the college adjoining the convent, next to the rooms of the inquisitor himself; and here I have been now four days at the very fountain-head of information, in regard to those subjects which I wished to investigate. I breakfast and dine with the inquisitor almost every day, and he generally passes his evenings in my apartment. As he considers my inquiries to be chiefly of a literary nature, he is perfectly candid and communicative on all subjects.

"Next day after my arrival, I was introduced by my learned conductor to the archbishop of Goa. We found him reading the Latin letters of St. Francis Xavier. On my adverting to the long duration of the city of Goa, while other cities of Europeans in India had suffered from war or revolution, the archbishop observed, that the preservation of Goa was 'owing to the prayers of St. Francis Xavier.' The inquisitor looked at me to see what I thought of this sentiment. I acknowledged that Xavier was considered by the learned among the English to have been a great man. What he wrote himself bespeaks him a man of learning, of original genius, and great fortitude of mind; but what others have written for him and of him has tarnished his fame, by making him the inventor of fables. The archbishop signified his assent. He afterwards conducted me into his private chapel, which is decorated with images of silver, and then into the archiepiscopal library, which possesses a valuable collection of books.—As I passed through our convent, in returning from the archbishop's, I observed among the paintings in the cloisters a portrait of the famous Alexis de Menezes, archbishop of Goa, who held the synod of Diamper near Cochin in 1599, and burned the books of the Syrian christians. From the inscription underneath, I learned that he was the founder of the magnificent church and convent in which I am now residing.

"On the same day I received an invitation to dine with the chief inquisitor, at his house in the country. The second inquisitor accompanied me, and we found a respectable company of priests, and a sumptuous entertainment. In the library of the chief inquisitor I saw a register, containing the present establishment of the inquisition at Goa, and the names of all the officers. On my asking the chief inquisitor whether the establishment was as extensive as formerly, he said it was nearly the same. I had hitherto said little to any person concerning the inquisition, but I had indirectly gleaned much information concerning it, not only from the inquisitors themselves, but from certain priests, whom I visited at their respective convents; particularly from a father in the Franciscan convent, who had himself repeatedly witnessed an Auto da Fe."

"*Goa, Augustinian Convent*, 26*th Jan.* 1808.

"On Sunday, after divine service, which I attended, we looked over together the prayers and portions of scripture for the day, which led to a discussion concerning some of the doctrines of christianity. We then read the third chapter of St. John's gospel, in the Latin vulgate. I asked the inquisitor whether he believed in the influence of the spirit there spoken of. He distinctly admitted it; conjointly however he thought, in some obscure sense, with *water*. I observed that water was merely an emblem of the purifying effects of the spirit, and could be *but* an emblem. We next adverted to the expression of St. John in his first Epistle; 'This is he that came by *water* and *blood:* even Jesus Christ; not by water only, but by water and blood:'—blood to atone for sin, and water to purify the heart; justification and sanctification: both of which were expressed at the same moment on the cross. The inquisitor was pleased with the subject. I referred to the evangelical doctrines of Augustin (we were now in the Augustinian convent) plainly asserted by that father in a thousand places, and he acknowledged their truth. I then asked him in what important doctrine he differed from the protestant church? He confessed that he never had a theological discussion with a protestant before. By an easy transition we passed to the importance of the Bible itself, to illuminate the priests and people. I noticed to him that after looking through the colleges and schools, there appeared to me to be a *total eclipse* of scriptural light. He acknowledged that religion and learning were truly in a degraded state.—I had visited the theological schools, and at every place I expressed my surprise to the tutors, in presence of the pupils, at the absence of the Bible, and almost total want of reference to it. They pleaded the custom of the place, and the scarcity of copies of the book itself. Some of the younger priests came to me afterwards, desiring to know by what means they might procure copies. This inquiry for Bibles was like a ray of hope beaming on the walls of the inquisition.

"I pass an hour sometimes in the spacious library of the Augustinian convent. There are many rare volumes, but they are chiefly theological, and almost all of the sixteenth century. There are few classics; and I have not yet seen one copy of the original scriptures in Hebrew or Greek."

"*Goa, Augustinian Convent, 27th Jan.* 1808.

"On the second morning after my arrival, I was surprised by my host, the inquisitor, coming into my apartment clothed in *black robes* from head to foot; for the usual dress of his order is white. He said he was going to sit on the tribunal of the holy office. 'I presume, father, your august office does not occupy much of your time.' 'Yes,' answered he, 'much; I sit on the tribunal three or four times every week.'

"I had thought, for some days, of putting Dellon's book into the inquisitor's hands; for if I could get him to advert to the facts stated in that book, I should be able to learn, by comparison, the exact state of the inquisition at the present time. In the evening he came in, as usual, to pass an hour in my apartment. After some conversation I took the pen in my hand to write a few notes in my journal; and, as if to amuse him, while I was writing, I took up Dellon's book, which was lying with some others on the table, and handing it across to him, asked him whether he had ever seen it. It was in the French language, which he understood well. 'Relation de l' inquisition de Goa,' pronounced he, with a slow, articulate voice. He had never seen it before, and began to read with eagerness. He had not proceeded far, before he betrayed evident symptoms of uneasiness. He turned hastily to the middle of the book, and then to the end, and then ran over the table of contents at the beginning, as if to ascertain the full extent of the evil. He then composed himself to read, while I continued to write. He turned over the pages with rapidity, and when he came to a certain place, he exclaimed in the broad Italian accent, 'Mendaçium, mendacium.' I requested he would mark those passages which were untrue, and we should discuss them afterwards, for that I had other books on the subject. 'Other books,' said he, and he looked with an enquiring eye on those on the table. He continued reading till it was time to retire to rest, and then begged to take the book with him.

"It was on this night that a circumstance happened which caused my first alarm at Goa. My servants slept every night at my chamber door, in the long gallery which is common to all the apartments, and not far distant from the servants of the convent. About midnight I was waked by loud shrieks and expressions of terror, from some person in the gallery. In the first moment of surprise I concluded it must be the *alguazils* of the holy office, seizing my servants to carry them to the inquisition; but, on going out, I saw my own servants standing at the door, and the person who had caused the alarm (a boy of about fourteen) at a little distance, surrounded by some of the priests, who had come out of their cells on hearing the noise. The boy said he had seen a *spectre*, and it was a considerable time before the agitations of his body and voice subsided.—Next morning at breakfast the inquisitor apologised for the disturbance, and said the boy's alarm proceeded from a 'phantasma animi,' a phantasm of the imagination.

"After breakfast we resumed the subject of the inquisition. The inquisitor admitted that Dellon's descriptions of the dungeons, of the torture, of the mode of trial, and of the Auto da Fe were, in general, just; but he said the writer judged untruly of the motives of the inquisitors, and very uncharitably of the character of the holy church; and I admitted that, under the pressure of his peculiar suffering, this might possibly be the case. The inquisitor was now anxious to know to what extent Dellon's book had been circulated in Europe. I told him that Picart had published to the world extracts from it, in his celebrated work called 'Religious Ceremonies;' together with plates of the system of torture and burnings at the Auto da Fe. I added that it was now generally believed in Europe that these enormities no longer existed, and that the inquisition itself had been totally suppressed; but that I was concerned to find that this was not the case. He now began a grave narration to show that the inquisition had undergone a change in some respects, and that its terrors were mitigated.'*

* The following were the passages in Mr. Dellon's narrative, to which I wished particularly to draw the attention of the inquisitor.—Mr. D. had been thrown into the inquisition at Goa, and confined in a dungeon, ten feet square, where he remained upwards of two years, without seeing any person, but the gaoler who brought him his victuals, except when he was brought to his trial, expecting daily to be brought to the stake. His alleged crime was, charging the inquisition with cruelty, in a conversation he had with a priest at Daman, another part of India.

"During the months of November and December, I heard, every morning, the shrieks of the unfortunate victims, who were undergoing the Question. I remembered to have heard, before I was cast into prison, that the Auto da Fe was generally celebrated on the first Sunday in Advent, because on that day is read in the churches that part of the gospel in which mention is made of the LAST JUDGMENT; and the inquisitors pretend by this ceremony to exhibit a lively emblem of that awful event. I was likewise convinced that there were a great number of prisoners, besides myself; the profound silence, which reigned within the walls of the building, having enabled me to count the number of doors which were opened at the hours of meals.—However, the first and second Sundays of Advent passed by, without my hearing of any thing, and I prepared to undergo another year of melancholy captivity, when I was aroused from my despair on the 11th of January, by the noise of the guards removing the bars from the door of my prison. The Alcaide presented me with a habit, which he ordered me to put on, and to make myself ready to attend him, when he should come again. Thus saying, he left a lighted lamp in my dungeon.—The guards returned, about two o'clock in the morning, and led me out into a long gallery, where I found a number of the companions of my fate, drawn up in a rank against a wall: I placed myself among the rest, and several more soon joined the melancholy band. The profound silence and stillness caused them to resemble statues more than the animated bodies of human creatures. The women, who were clothed in a similar manner, were placed in a neighbouring gallery, where we could not see them; but I remarked that a number of persons stood by themselves at some distance, attended by others who wore long black dresses, and who walked backwards and forwards occasionally. I did not then know who these were; but I was afterwards informed that the former were the victims who were condemned to be burned, and the others were their confessors."

"After we were all ranged against the wall of this gallery, we received each a large wax taper. They then brought us a number of dresses made of yellow cloth, with the cross of St. Andrew painted before and behind. This is called the San Benito. The relapsed heretics wear another species of robe, called the Samarra, the ground of which is grey. The portrait of the sufferer is painted upon it, placed upon burning torches with flames and demons all round.—Caps were then produced called Carrochas; made of pasteboard, pointed like sugar-loaves, all covered with devils and flames of fire."

"The great bell of the cathedral began to ring a little before sun-rise, which served as a signal to warn the people of Goa to come and behold the august ceremony of the Auto da Fe; and then they made us proceed from the gallery one by one. I remarked as we passed into the great hall that the inquisitor was sitting at the door with his secretary by him, and that he delivered every prisoner into the hands of a particular person, who is to be his guard to the place of burning. These persons are called Parrains, or godfathers. My godfather was the commander of a ship. I went forth with him, and as soon as we were in the street, I saw that the procession was commenced by the Dominican friars; who have this honour, because St. Dominic founded the inquisition. These are followed by the prisoners, who walk one after the other, each having his godfather by his side, and a lighted taper in his hand. The least guilty go foremost; and as I did not pass for one of them, there were many who took precedence of me. The women were mixed promiscuously with the men. We all walked barefoot, and the sharp stones of the streets of Goa wounded my tender feet, and caused the blood to stream; for they made

"I had already discovered, from written or printed documents, that the inquisition at Goa was suppressed by royal edict, in the year 1775, and established again in 1779. The Franciscan father before mentioned witnessed the annual Auto da Fe, from 1770 to 1775. 'It was the humanity, and tender mercy of a good king,' said the old father, 'which abolished the inquisition.' But immediately on his death, the power of the priests acquired the ascendant, under the queen dowager, and the tribunal was re-established, after a bloodless interval of five years. It has continued in operation ever since. It was restored in 1779, subject to certain restrictions, the chief of which are the two following, 'That a greater number of witnesses should be required to convict a criminal than were before necessary;' and, 'That the Auto da Fe should not be held publicly as before; but that the sentences of the tribunal should be executed privately, within the walls of the inquisition.'

"In this particular, the constitution of the new inquisition is more reprehensible than that of the old one; for, as the old father expressed it, 'Nunc sigillum non revelat inquisitio.'—Formerly the friends of those unfortunate persons who were thrown into its prison, had the

us march through the chief streets of the city; and we were regarded everywhere by an innumerable crowd of people, who had assembled from all parts of India to behold this spectacle; for the inquisition takes care to announce it long before, in the most remote parishes. At length we arrived at the church of St. Francis, which was, for this time, destined for the celebration of the Act of Faith. On one side of the altar was the grand inquisitor and his counsellors; and on the other, the viceroy of Goa and his court. All the prisoners are seated to hear a sermon. I observed that those prisoners who wore the horrible Carrochas came in last in the procession. One of the Augustin monks ascended the pulpit, and preached for a quarter of an hour. The sermon being concluded, two readers went up to the pulpit, one after the other, and read the sentences of the prisoners. My joy was extreme, when I heard that my sentence was not to be burnt, but to be a galley-slave for five years.—After the sentences were read, they summoned forth those miserable victims who were destined to be immolated by the holy inquisition. The images of the heretics who had died in prison were brought up at the same time, their bones being contained in small chests covered with flames and demons.—An officer of the secular tribunal now came forward, and seized these unhappy people, after they had each received a slight blow upon the breast, from the alcaide, to intimate that they were abandoned. They were then led away to the bank of the river, where the viceroy and his court were assembled, and where the faggots had been prepared the preceding day.—As soon as they arrive at this place, the condemned persons are asked in what religion they choose to die; and the moment they have replied to this question, the executioner seizes them, and binds them to a stake in the midst of the faggots. The day after the execution, the portraits of the dead are carried to the church of the Dominicans. The heads only are represented, (which are generally very accurately drawn; for the inquisition keeps excellent limners for the purpose,) surrounded by flames and demons; and underneath is the name and crime of the person who has been burned."—Relation de l'Inquisition de Goa, chap. XXIV.

melancholy satisfaction of seeing them once a year walking in the procession of the Auto da Fe; or if they were condemned to die, they witnessed their death, and mourned for the dead. But now they have no means of learning for years whether they be dead or alive. The policy of this new code of concealment appears to be this, to preserve the power of the inquisition, and at the same time to lessen the public odium of its proceedings, in the presence of British dominion and civilization. I asked the father his opinion concerning the nature and frequency of the punishments within the walls. He said he possessed no certain means of giving a satisfactory answer; that every thing transacted there was declared to be 'sacrum et secretum.' But this he knew to be true, that there were constantly captives in the dungeons; that some of them are liberated after long confinement, but that they never speak afterwards of what passed within the place. He added that, of all the persons he had known, who had been liberated, he never knew one who did not carry about with him what might be called, 'the mark of the inquisition;' that is to say, who did not show in the solemnity of his countenance, or in his peculiar demeanour, or his terror of the priests, that he had been in that dreadful place.

"The chief argument of the inquisitor to prove the melioration of the inqisition was the superior *humanity* of the inqisitors. I remarked that I did not doubt the humanity of the existing officers; but what availed humanity in an inquisitor? he must pronounce sentence according to the laws of the tribunal, which are notorious enough; and a *relapsed heretic* must be burned in the flames, or confined for life in a dungeon, whether the inquisitor be humane or not. But if, said I, you would satisfy my mind completely on this subject, 'show me the inquisition.' He said it was not permitted to any person to see the inquisition. I observed that mine might be considered as a peculiar case; that the character of the inquisition, and the expediency of its longer continuance had been called in question; that I had myself written on the civilization of India, and might possibly publish something more upon that subject, and that it could not be expected that I should pass over the inquisition without notice, knowing what I did of its proceedings; at the same time I should not wish to state a single fact without his authority, or at least his admission of its truth. I added that he himself had been pleased to communicate with me very fully on the subject, and that in all our discussions we had both been actuated, I hoped, by a good purpose. The countenance of the inquisitor evidently altered on receiving this intimation, nor did it ever after wholly regain its wonted frankness and placidity. After some hesitation, however, he said, he would take me with him to the inquisition the next day.—I was a good deal surprised at this acquiescence of the inquisitor, but I did not know what was in his mind.

"Next morning after breakfast my host went to dress for the holy office, and soon returned in his inquisitorial robes. He said he would go half an hour before the usual time for the purpose of showing me the inquisition. The buildings are about a quarter of a mile distant from the convent, and we proceeded thither in our *manjeels*.* On our arrival at the place, the inquisitor said to me, as we were ascending the steps of the outer stair, that he hoped I should be satisfied with a transient view of the inquisition, and that I would retire whenever he should desire it. I took this as a good omen, and followed my conductor with tolerable confidence.

"He led me first to the great hall of the inquisition. We were met at the door by a number of well dressed persons, who, I afterwards understood, were the familiars, and attendants of the holy office. They bowed very low to the inquisitor, and looked with surprise at me. The great hall is the place in which the prisoners are marshalled for the procession of the Auto da Fe. At the procession described by Dellon, in which he himself walked barefoot, clothed with the painted garment, there were upwards of one hundred and fifty prisoners. I traversed this hall for some time, with a slow step, reflecting on its former scenes, the inquisitor walking by my side in silence. I thought of the fate of the multitude of my fellow-creatures who had passed through this

* The manjeel is a kind of palankeen common at Goa. It is merely a sea cot suspended from a bamboo, which is borne on the heads of four men. Sometimes a footman runs before, having a staff in his hand, to which are attached little bells or rings, which he jingles as he runs, keeping time with the motion of the bearers.

place, condemned by a tribunal of their fellow-sinners, their bodies devoted to the flames, and their souls to perdition. And I could not help saying to him, 'Would not the holy church wish, in her mercy, to have those souls back again, that she might allow them a little further probation?' The inquisitor answered nothing, but beckoned me to go with him to a door at one end of the hall. By this door he conducted me to some small rooms, and thence to the spacious apartments of the chief inquisitor. Having surveyed these, he brought me back again to the great hall; and I thought he seemed now desirous that I should depart. 'Now, father,' said I, 'lead me to the dungeons below; I want to see the captives.'—'No,' said he, 'that cannot be.'—I now began to suspect that it had been in the mind of the inquisitor, from the beginning, to show me only a certain part of the inquisition, in the hope of satisfying my inquiries in a general way. I urged him with earnestness, but he steadily resisted, and seemed to be offended, or rather agitated, by my importunity. I intimated to him plainly, that the only way to do justice to his own assertions and arguments, regarding the present state of the inquisition, was to show me the prisons and the captives. I should then describe only what I saw; but now the subject was left in awful obscurity.—'Lead me down,' said I, 'to the inner building, and let me pass through the two hundred dungeons, ten feet square, described by your former captives. Let me count the number of your present captives, and converse with them. I want to see if there be any subjects of the British government, to whom we owe protection. I want to ask how long they have been here, how long it is since they beheld the light of the sun, and whether they ever expect to see it again. Show me the chamber of torture; and declare what modes of execution, or of punishment, are now practised within the walls of the inquisition, in lieu of the public Auto da Fe. If, after all that has passed, father, you resist this reasonable request, I shall be justified in believing, that you are afraid of exposing the real state of the inquisition in India.' To these observations the inquisitor made no reply; but seemed impatient that I should withdraw. 'My good father,' said I, 'I am about to take my leave of you, and to thank you for your hospitable attentions, (it had been before understood that I should take my final leave at the door of the inquisition, after having seen the interior,) and I wish always to preserve on my mind a favourable sentiment of your kindness and candour. You cannot, you say, show me the captives and the dungeons; be pleased then merely to answer this question, for I shall believe your word:—How many prisoners are there now below, in the cells of the inquisition?' The inquisitor replied, 'That is a question which I cannot answer.' On his pronouncing these words, I retired hastily towards the door, and wished him farewell. We shook hands with as much cordiality as we could at the moment assume; and both of us, I believe, were sorry that our parting took place with a clouded countenance.

"From the inquisition I went to the place of burning in the *Campo Santo Lazaro*, on the river side, where the victims were brought to the stake at the Auto da Fe. It is close to the palace, that the viceroy and his court may witness the execution; for it has ever been the policy of the inquisition to make these spiritual executions appear to be the executions of the state. An old priest accompanied me, who pointed out the place and described the scene. As I passed over this melancholy plain, I thought on the difference between the pure and benign doctrine, which was first preached to India in the apostolic age, and that bloody code, which after a long night of darkness, was announced to it under the same name! And I pondered on the mysterious dispensation, which permitted the ministers of the inquisition, with their racks and flames, to visit these lands, before the heralds of the gospel of peace. But the most painful reflection was, that this tribunal should yet exist, unawed by the vicinity of British humanity and dominion. I was not satisfied with what I had seen or said at the inquisition, and I determined to go back again. The inquisitors were now sitting on the tribunal, and I had some excuse for returning; for I was to receive from the chief inquisitor a letter which he said he would give me, before I left the place, for the British resident in Travancore, being an answer to a letter from that officer.

"When I arrived at the inquisition, and had ascended the outer stairs, the door-keepers surveyed me doubtingly, but suffered me to pass, supposing that I had returned by permission and appointment of the inquisitor. I entered the great hall, and went up directly towards the tribunal of the inquisition, described by Dellon, in which is the lofty crucifix. I sat down on a form, and wrote some notes; and then desired one of the attendants to carry in my name to the inquisitor. As I walked up the hall, I saw a poor woman sitting by herself, on a bench by the wall, apparently in a disconsolate state of mind. She clasped her hands as I passed, and gave me a look expressive of her distress. This sight chilled my spirits. The familiars told me she was waiting there to be called up before the tribunal of the inquisition. While I was asking questions concerning her crime, the second inquisitor came out in evident trepidation, and was about to complain of the intrusion; when I informed him I had come back for the letter from the chief inquisitor. He said it should be sent after me to Goa; and he conducted me with a quick step towards the door. As we passed the poor woman, I pointed to her, and said with some emphasis, 'Behold, father, another victim of the holy inquisition!' He answered nothing. When we arrived at the head of the great stair, he bowed, and I took my last leave of Josephus a Doloribus, without uttering a word."

The foregoing particulars concerning the inquisition at Goa are detailed chiefly with this view; that the English nation may consider, whether there be sufficient ground for presenting a remonstrance to the Portuguese government, on the longer continuance of that tribunal in India; it being notorious, that a great part of the Romish christians are now under British protection. "The Romans," says Montesquieu, "deserved well of human nature, for making it an article in their treaty with the Carthagenians, that they should abstain from SACRIFICING their CHILDREN to their gods." It has been lately observed by respectable writers, that the English nation ought to imitate this example, and endeavour to induce her allies "to abolish the human sacrifices of the inquisition;" and a censure is passed on our government for their indifference to this subject.* The indifference to the inquisition is attributable, we believe, to the same cause which has produced an indifference to the religious principles which first organized the inquisition. The mighty despot, who suppressed the inquisition in Spain, was not swayed probably by very powerful motives of humanity; but viewed with jealousy a tribunal, which usurped an independent dominion; and he put it down, on the same principle that he put down the popedom, that he might remain pontiff and grand inquisitor himself. And so he will remain for a time, till the purposes of Providence shall have been accomplished by him. But are we to look on in silence, and to expect that further meliorations in human society are to be effected by despotism, or by great revolutions? —"If," say the same authors, "while the inquisition is destroyed in Europe by the power of despotism, we could entertain the hope, and it is not too much to entertain such a hope, that the power of liberty is about to destroy it in America; we might even, amid the gloom that surrounds us, congratulate our fellow-creatures on one of the most remarkable periods in the history of the progress of human society, the FINAL ERASURE *of the inquisition from the face of the earth*,"† It will indeed be an important and happy day to the earth, when this final erasure shall take place; but the period of such an event is nearer, I apprehend, in Europe and America, than it is in Asia; and its termination in Asia depends as much on Great Britain as on Portugal. And shall not Great Britain do her part to hasten this desirable time? Do we wait, as if to see whether the power of infidelity will abolish the other inquisitions of the earth? Shall not we, in the mean while, attempt to do something, on christian principles, for the honour of God and of humanity? Do we dread even to express a sentiment on the subject in our legislative assemblies, or to notice it in our treaties? It is surely our duty to declare our wishes, at least, for the abolition of these inhuman tribunals, (since we take an active part in promoting the welfare of other nations,) and to deliver our testimony against them in the presence of Europe.

This case is not unlike that of the immolation of females; with this aggravation in regard to the latter,

* Edin. Rev. No. XXXII. p. 429. † Ibid.

that the rite is perpetrated in our own territories. Our humanity revolts at the occasional description of the enormity; but the matter comes not to our own business and bosoms, and we fail even to insinuate our disapprobation of the deed. It may be concluded then, that while we remain silent and unmoved spectators of the flames of the widow's pile, there is no hope that we shall be justly affected by the reported horrors of the inquisition.

TRANSLATIONS OF THE SCRIPTURES FOR THE ROMISH CHRISTIANS.

The principal languages spoken by the Romish christians in India are these four; the Tamul, the Malabar, the Ceylonese, and the Portuguese. The author has already had occasion to notice the three first. The Tamul version has been long since completed by the Protestant missionaries; and the Malabar and the Ceylonese are in course of publication.—It is now proper to explain, that excellent effects may be expected from the diffusion of the *Portuguese* scriptures in India. The Portuguese language prevails wherever there are, or *have been*, settlements of that nation. Their descendants people the coasts from the vicinity of the Cape of Good Hope to the sea of China; beginning from Sofala, Mocaranga, Mosambique, (where there is a bishop,) Zinzebar, and Melinda, (where there are many churches,) on the east of Africa; and extending round by Babelmandel, Diu, Surat, Daman, Bombay, Goa, Calicut, Cochin, Angengo, Tutecorin, Negapatam, Jaffna-patam, Columbo, Point de Galle, Tranquebar, Tanjore, Tritchinopoly, Porto-Novo, Pondicherry, Sadras, Madras, Masulipatam, Calcutta, Chinsurah, Bandel, Chittagong, Macao, and Canton; and almost all the islands of the Malayan Archipelago, which were first conquered by the Portuguese. The greater part of the Portuguese in India are now subjects of the British empire. The author visited most of the places above enumerated; and in many of them he could not hear of a single copy of the Portuguese scriptures. There is a Portuguese press at Tranquebar, and another at Vespery near Madras; and pecuniary aid only is wanted from Europe to multiply copies, and to circulate them round the coasts of Asia. The Portuguese language is certainly a most favourable medium for diffusing the true religion in the maritime provinces of the east.

THE COLLEGES AT GOA.

Goa will probably remain the theological school to a great part of India, for a long period to come. It is of vast importance to the interests of christianity in the east, that this source of instruction should be purified. The appointed instrument for effecting this, is the Bible. This is "the salt which must be thrown into the fountain to heal the waters."* There are upwards of three thousand priests belonging to Goa, who are resident at the place, or stationed with their cures at a distance. Let us send the holy scriptures to illuminate the priests of Goa. It was distinctly expressed to the author, by several authorities, that they will gladly receive copies of the Latin and Portuguese vulgate Bible from the hands of the English nation.

THE PERSIANS.

The christian religion flourished very generally in Persia till about A. D. 651; when, the Persians being subdued by the Saracens, Mahomedanism gradually acquired the predominance. Constantine the Great, addressed a letter to Sapor, king of Persia, which is preserved to this day, recommending the christian churches in his dominions, to his protection; and a bishop from Persia was present at the council of Nice in A. D. 325. It appears also that there was a translation of some portion of the scriptures into the Persian language at that period; for we are informed by Chrysostom that, "the Persians, having translated the doctrines of the gospel

* 2 Kings ii. 21.

into their own tongue, had learned, though barbarians, the true philosophy;"* and it is stated by another author in the following century, "That the Hebrew writings were not only translated into the Greek, but into the Latin, Ethiopian, *Persian*, Indian, Armenian, Scythian, and Sarmatian languages."†

In the beautiful homily of Chrysostom on Mary's memorial, preached about A. D. 380, in which he enumerates those nations, who, in fulfilment of our Saviour's prophecy, had "spoken of the deed of Mary for a memorial of her," he mentions the *Persians* first, and the Isles of *Britain* last. "The Persians, Indians, Scythians, Thracians, Sarmatians, the race of the Moors, and the inhabitants of the British Isles, celebrate a deed performed in a private family in Judea by a woman that had been a harlot,"‡ "pouring an alabaster box of spikenard on the head of Christ," thereby acknowledging him, while yet upon earth, as God's ANOINTED King, and embalming his body, (as our Lord himself explained it) in anticipation of his burial; concerning which act of faith and love he uttered the following prophetic declaration: "Verily, I say unto you, Wheresoever this gospel shall be preached throughout the whole world, THIS also that she hath done shall be spoken of for a MEMORIAL of her." Mark xiv. 9.—The Isles of Britain are now the *first* to restore this memorial, and the gospel which recites it, to the Persians as well as to other Mahomedan nations, who were to lose it generally, during the great prophetic period of 1260 years.

A version of the four Gospels into the Persian language of a former age remains to this day. It is a faithful translation, and seems to have been made immediately from the Syriac;§ but the dialect and orthography are so ancient as to be scarcely intelligible even at Isfahan. The Romish church has had several missions

* Chrysostom, Hom. II. in Johan.

† Theodoret, vol. iv. p. 555. We have entirely lost sight of some of these versions in the obscurity of Mahomedan darkness. It is not even known what languages are intended by the Scythian, Indian, and Sarmatian. The christian church must now retrace her steps, and endeavour to recover a knowledge which she has lost.

‡ Chrysostom saith that nothing could have given so permanent a celebrity to so private an occurrence, but the divine word of HIM who foretold it. He supposes the woman to have been Mary Magdalene, but probably she was Mary, the sister of Martha.

§ This is the version of the Polyglot.

in the kingdom of Persia for some centuries past. The Augustinian mission from Goa commenced in the year 1602, "and was permitted by Sultan Murad to build convents in all parts of the empire."* But they went into Persia, as into other countries, not with the design of instructing men in the holy scriptures, but of teaching them the tenets and ceremonies of Rome. To this day, they have not published, under all the advantages of toleration which they enjoyed, a translation of the Bible, or even of the New Testament, into the Persian language.

It is a reproach to christians, that the only endeavour to produce a translation of the scriptures into the language of that extensive kingdom should have been made by the Persians themselves. The representatives of the christian churches in Europe, of every denomination, may well blush, when they read the following authentic relation of an attempt made by a Persian king to procure a knowledge of our religion.

"Towards the close of the year 1740, Nadir Shah caused a translation of the four Evangelists to be made into Persian.—The affair was put under the direction of Mirza Mehdee, a man of some learning, who, being vested with proper authority for the purpose, summoned several Armenian bishops, and priests, together with divers missionaries of the Romish church, and Persian Mullahs† to meet him at Isfahan. As to the latter, the Mahomedan priests, they could not be gainers, since the change of religion, if any, was to be in prejudice of Mahomedanism. Besides, Nadir's conduct towards them had been severe, to an extreme and unprecedented degree; many of them therefore gave Mirza Mehdee large bribes to excuse their absence. Among the christians summoned on this occasion, only one Romish priest, a native of Persia, was a sufficient master of the language to enter upon a work of so critical a nature. As to the Armenian christians, although they are born subjects to Persia, and intermixed with the inhabitants, yet are there very few of them who understand the language fundamentally. It was natural to expect that Mirza Mehdee, and the Persian Mullahs, would be more solicitous to please Nadir, and to support the credit of

* Fabricii Lux Evan. p. 639. † Mahomedan priests.

Mahomedanism, than to divest themselves of prejudices, and become masters of so important a subject. This translation was dressed up with all the glosses which the fables of the Koran could warrant. Their chief guide was an *ancient Arabic and Persian translation.* Father de Vignes, a Romish priest, was also employed in this work, in which he made use of the vulgate edition. They were but six months in completing this translation, and transcribing several fair copies of it.

"In May following, Mirza Mehdee with the Persian Mullahs and some of the christian priests set out from Isfahan for the Persian court, which was then held in encampment near Teheran. Nadir received them with some marks of civility, and had a cursory view of the performance. Some part of it was read to him; on which occasion he made several ludicrous remarks on the mysterious parts of the christian religion; at the same time he laughed at the Jews, and turned Mahomed and Ali equally into ridicule."—And after some expressions of levity, intimating that he could himself make a better religion than any that had yet been produced, "he dismissed these churchmen and translators with some small presents, not equal in value to the expense of the journey."*

This version of the gospels, prepared by command of Nadir Shah, is probably the same with that which is sometimes found in the hands of the Armenian priests in India. A copy was lately shown to an oriental scholar in Bengal,† who observed, "that if this was the same, he did not wonder at Nadir's contempt of it."

The number of natives already professing christianity in Persia, and who are prepared to receive a translation of the scriptures, is very considerable. They consist of four or five classes, viz. the Georgian, the Armenian, the Nestorian, the Jacobite, and the Romish christians. The *Georgians* have the Bible in the Georgian language, which was printed at Moscow in 1743; but the language is not so generally cultivated among the higher ranks as the Persian. It probably bears the same relation to the Persian, which the Welch does to the English. The *Armenians* have a version of the Bible in their own proper tongue, but the copies are few in number. The

* Hanway's Travels. † Rev. H. Martyn.

Nestorian and *Jacobite* christians use the Syriac Bible; but it is yet more rare than the Armenian. There are, besides, multitudes of *Jews* in Persia, who, as well as these different classes of christians, commonly speak the vernacular language of the country.

The Persian language is known far beyond the limits of Persia proper. It is spoken at all the Mussulman courts in India, and is the usual language of judicial proceedings under the British government in Hindostan. It is next in importance to the Arabic and Chinese, in regard to the extent of territory through which it is spoken, being generally understood from Calcutta to Damascus.

Here then is a language, spoken over nearly one quarter of the globe, the proper tongue of a great kingdom, in which an attempt has already been made by royal authority to obtain a translation of the christian scriptures; and where there are, at a low computation, two hundred thousand christians ready to receive them. Many of the Persians themselves would read the Bible with avidity, if presented to them in an inviting form. The cause of the little jealousy of christianity in Persia, compared with that which is found in other Mahomedan states, is to be ascribed to these two circumstances; first, That christianity has always existed in Persia, the christian natives forming a considerable part of the population; and secondly, That the Persians themselves profess so lax a system of Islamism that they have been accounted by some Mussulmans a kind of heretics.

It will form an epoch in the history of Persia, when a version of the Old and New Testaments shall begin to be known generally in that country. But the narrative of Nadir Shah's attempt sufficiently proves that no ordinary scholar is qualified to undertake it. The author of such a translation must be a perfect master of the Arabic language, the mother of the Persic, and familiar with the popular and classical Persian. He must, moreover, have access to the scriptures in their *original* tongues. Such a person, we think, has been found in SABAT of Arabia, who is accounted, by competent judges, "to be the first Arabic scholar of the age."* He has been employed for nearly four years past in translating the

* See Report of Translations by Rev. Henry Martyn, hereafter quoted.

scriptures into the Persian and Arabic languages, in conjunction with Mirza Filrut of Lucknow, and other learned natives. Mirza is himself a Persian by descent, and a man of liberal learning among his countrymen. He visited England some years ago, and was afterwards appointed a Persian teacher, and a translator of the scriptures in the college of Fort-William. These versions by Sabat and Mirza, are conducted under the superintendence of the Rev. Henry Martyn, who is himself an Arabic and Persian scholar, and skilled in the *original* tongues of the sacred scriptures. He is a chaplain to the honourable the East India Company, and is now stationed at Cawnpore in Bengal, where his learned coadjutors also reside. The gospels of St. Matthew and St. Luke, translated by Sabat into the Persian language, have already been printed; and 800 copies are stated in the last report, dated May 1810, to have been deposited in the BIBLIOTHECA BIBLICA, at Calcutta, for sale.

THE ARABIANS.

ARABIA was the country in which St. Paul first opened his heavenly ministry. "When it pleased God," saith that apostle, "who called me by his grace, to reveal his Son in me, that I might preach him among the heathen; immediately I conferred not with flesh and blood; neither went I up to Jerusalem, but I went into ARABIA." Gal. i. 17. Christianity flourished very extensively in Arabia, during the first centuries. History informs us, that "the disciples of Christ had filled its provinces with the churches of God;"* and frequent mention is made, in the early monuments, of the bishops of Arabia.† This early influence of the gospel in that region might be expected; for Arabia adjoins Palestine; and the climate of the country, and the manners and customs of the people, are nearly the same.‡

* Procopius Gaz. Ex. XI. 14.

† See them enumerated in Beveridge's 'Canones Conciliorum.' The bishop of Busorah was present at the council of Antioch in A. D. 269.

‡ Being neighbours to the Jews, it was likely that they should first receive the gospel. Proc. ubi supra.

There are some circumstances which remarkably distinguish Arabia; a recollection of which, in connexion with others, ought now to draw our attention to it. Arabia was inhabited by the first generations of men. There it pleased the Creator first to reveal himself to his creatures; and in its vicinity the Son of God assumed the human nature. In Arabia, the faculties of the human mind attain to as high a degree of strength and vigour, even at this day,* as in any other country in the world; and the symmetry and beauty of the human person in Arabia are not surpassed by any other portion of the human race.†

Arabia is also remarkable on another account. It was the theatre of the grand defection from christianity, by the Mahomedan delusion, which was to extend to "a third part of men." This predicted apostacy was to be effected, not by returning to paganism, but by a corruption of christianity; that is, by admitting some part of the former revelation of God, and pretending to a new revelation. The delusion itself is aptly compared in the prophecy concerning it, to "*smoke* issuing from the bottomless pit;" and its great extent is expressed by its "darkening the *sun* and the *air*."‡ And since this defection was to be produced by a corruption of revealed truth, it was necessary that the *scriptures* should be first corrupted; for where the genuine scriptures are in the hands of men, there is little danger of general infidelity. Accordingly, this preparative for the great imposture took place in the fifth and sixth centuries. During that

* See letter from the Rev. Henry Martyn, concerning Sabat, quoted in "The Star in the East," p. 218. "At intervals I read Persian poetry with Mirza, and the Koran with Sabat. These Orientals, with whom I translate the scriptures, require me to point out the connexion between every two sentences, which is often more than I can do. It is curious how accurately they observe all the rules of writing. Sabat, though a real christian, has not lost a jot of his Arabian notions of superiority. He looks upon Europeans as mushrooms; and seems to regard my pretensions to any learning, as we should regard those of a savage or an ape."—N. B. Mr. Martyn was senior wrangler, or first mathematician of his year, at Cambridge, in 1801; and he had now been two years in society with Sabat.

† An intelligent Arabian, who had seen the English in India, observed to the author, that he thought the minds of the English far superior to their persons. It seemed to him, that there was nothing striking or noble in the English countenance, compared with the dignity and beauty of the Arabians; that the faces were in general flat and torpid, and the eyes without fire. The author informed him, that the English were composed of different nations, and most of these from cold and northern climates; that hence there was a great diversity in their appearance, some being of very ordinary aspect, and others of a dignity and beauty which even an Arabian would admire.

‡ Rev. ix. 2.

period, corrupt and apocryphal gospels prevailed so generally in Arabia and in the neighbouring regions, that it is even doubtful whether Mahomed himself ever saw a genuine copy of the New Testament. It has been argued by learned men, from the internal evidence of his composition, that he did not. But now even the apocryphal gospels have vanished from view, by the long prevalence of the Koran.

But the duration of this delusion was to have a limit. "The smoke was to darken the sun and the air" only for a definite period. This period is expressed in prophetic scripture in a *three-fold* form of words to evince its certainty.

1. "The Holy City shall they tread under foot *forty and two months.*"* Rev. xi. 2.—This marks the period of the *Mahomedan* power. The same expression is applied afterwards to the duration of the *Papal* power. The depression of the true faith was of course to last the same time; as expressed in the two following sentences.

2. "The Witnesses (for the true faith) shall prophesy a *thousand two hundred and three score days,* clothed in sackloth."† Rev. xi. 3.

3. "The Woman (or church of Christ) fled into the wilderness, and was nourished for a *time, times* and *half a time.*"‡ Rev. xii. 14.

This last expression, "a time, times and half a time," is also used by the prophet Daniel, who foretels the same events, to mark the period when God shall "have accomplished to scatter the power of the holy people," and shall terminate his indignation against *Israel.* Dan. xii. 7.

It is very well known in the east at what time Mahomed appeared. Let the Mahomedan then be informed, that he is to count 1260 years from the Hejira, and then expect the fulfilment of a remarkable prophecy, made by Christ, whom the Koran acknowledges to be "a true prophet." Let him be informed explicitly, that the reign of Mahomedanism will then have an end. And, if he be unwilling to believe this, ask him if he does not

* A day for a year;
42 months = 42 × 30 = 1260 days . . . . . = 1260 years.
† A day for a year; 1260 days . . . . = 1260 years.
‡ A time, times and half a time = a year, two years, and half of a year = forty-two months = 1260 days . . = 1260 years.

already perceive the *decline* of Mahomedanism. If he be ignorant of this fact, inform him of the history of events. Instruct him, that the corruption of christianity in the west by the pope, was coeval with the corruption of christianity in the east by Mahomed, that the decline of both these powers is, at this time, equally advanced; and that the fall of both is to be contemporaneous. If he be ignorant of the decline of papal Rome, the Roman catholic in the east will declare it to him.

Is there any man, calling himself a christian, who thinks that these prophecies are dubious? If it be true that God hath, at any time, revealed himself to man, they are most certain. The author would here observe, that the inattention of men in general to the fulfilment of the divine predictions, does not proceed so commonly from principles of infidelity as from ignorance of *facts*,—pure ignorance of historical facts. There are men of liberal education in England, who are more ignorant of the history of the world, ancient and modern, *in connexion with the revelation of God*, than some Hindoos and Arabians, whom we know in the east, who have not been christians above a few years. Our Saviour reprehended this neglect of "the word spoken from heaven" in these words; "ye can discern the face of the sky and of the earth; but how is it that ye cannot discern THIS TIME?" Luke xii. 56.

The author has noticed the foregoing circumstances in connexion with Arabia, to illustrate the importance of preparing a version of the scriptures for that country, at the present era. But the Arabic language hath gone forth far beyond the bounds of Arabia, and is known to almost "a third part of men" in the east. The Koran has consecrated it in the eyes of millions, in central Asia, on the continent of Africa, and in the isles of the Indian Ocean.

A version of the whole Bible in Arabic has come down to us; but it is now antiquated, like the Persian, both in dialect and orthography. It does not appear that any composition in a living language, of a higher date than about five hundred years, can be of popular use, unless we learn it from our infancy. The language of our own scriptures becomes now peculiar in many respects, and distinct from the popular speech. It is supposed that the Arabic translation is upwards of a thousand years old. Had there been no interruption in the profession of christianity in Arabia, the ancient translation might possibly have sufficed; in like manner as the Hebrew is still understood by the Jews, and the Syriac by the Syrian christians. But when a new religion is to be proposed to a people, we must use the most dignified medium, and present it in the language which is in popular use. The present Arabic translation in the Polyglot is perfectly intelligible to those who will study it with a lexicon; but we certainly cannot offer it at this time as conveying the meaning of the christian scriptures to the land of Yemen, or Arabia the Happy.

Soon after Sabat, the Arabian, had been converted to christianity,* the object which chiefly occupied his thoughts, was a translation of the scriptures for his native country. He himself could easily read and understand the existing translation; for he is a learned man, and acquainted radically with every dialect of the language; and it was by means of that translation that he himself became a christian;† but he says he should be ashamed to offer the Bible to his countrymen in its present form; such a version would neither be acceptable to the learned, nor intelligible to the unlearned.

This noble Arabian has been now three years, or more, employed in translating the scriptures into the Arabic language, with the aid of other learned Asiatics, under the superintendence of the Rev. H. Martyn, who has himself been long a student of the Arabic tongue. Mr. Martyn has lately stated their reasons for undertaking a new translation, which the author will here subjoin, in deference to the learned at home, who may think some further explanation necessary.

"Of the Arabic version of the Polyglot, the late Professor Carlyle, in his copy of proposals for printing a new edition of it, speaks in the highest terms, and ob-

* See an account of his conversion in "The Star in the East."

† The copy of the New Testament, which fell into the hands of Sabat, was one of the edition published in 1727 by "the Society for promoting Christian Knowledge," revised by Salomon Negri. An investment of these Arabic Testaments was sent about 1759, to the Society's missionaries in Calcutta, who circulated them through different provinces. The following is a well-attested fact: They sent some copies to the Mahomedan priests at Delhi, who "requested that the supply might be continued." See proceedings of the Society of that period.

serves, that it was used both by Jews and Christians as a faithful and elegant representation of their respective books of faith. But even supposing that both Jews and Christians are satisfied with the translation, no one, who has had an opportunity of observing the degraded state of these people in the east, would admit them as competent judges of the Arabic. The professor has adduced, in favour of the version in question, the opinions of Erpenius, Gabriel Sionita, and Pocock; names of high consideration in Arabic learning, particularly the last. It is certain, however, that such of the Mahomedans as have seen this version, think very differently of it. If we would invite the fastidious Mussulman to review the sacred law which he supposes abrogated, let us not neglect our present opportunities; but, with such an instrument as Sabat in our possession, let us attempt at least, to send forth the scriptures in a style which shall command respect, even in Nujed and Hejaz."

Mr. Martyn adverts to the new edition of the Polyglot translation, now publishing in England, under the patronage of the bishop of Durham, and highly commends the design. "We rejoice," writes he, "to hear that the old Polyglot is going forth at last in a new dress. It may be useful to some in Asia, as it was to Sabat." —And, in regard to the extent of country through which the Arabic is spoken, he observes, that the Arabic translation is of more importance than one-fourth of all the translations now in hand. "We will begin," says he, "to preach to Arabia, Syria, Persia, Tartary, part of India and of China, half of Africa, all the sea-coast of the Mediterranean and Turkey; and one tongue shall suffice for them all."

The proposal for publishing the Arabic Bible has already met with a very liberal patronage in India. It is intended to publish an edition of the New Testament, in a splendid form, for the use of the chief men in Arabia and Persia, resembling, as nearly as possible, their own beautiful writing. The universities, and literary bodies in Europe, will, no doubt, be disposed to subscribe for some copies of this truly classical work. It is stated in the last accounts, dated May 1810, that the translation of the New Testament was expected to be finished by the end of the present year, 1811.

THE ARABIC SCHOOL

FOR THE

TRANSLATION OF THE SCRIPTURES.

THE Rev. Henry Martyn, B. D. Fellow of St. John's College, Cambridge, went out to India about five years ago. His qualifications for the general superintendence of scriptural translation, are truly respectable. After acquiring the highest academical honours in science, and a just celebrity for classical knowledge, he devoted himself to the acquirement of the Arabic and Hindostanee languages. His mind was strongly impressed, at an early period, with the duty and importance of communicating the revealed religion to heathen nations. He had a spirit to follow the steps of Swartz and Brainerd, and preach to the natives in the woods; but his peculiar qualifications, as a critical scholar, have fixed him to the department of translation. He had not been long in Bengal before he was joined by Sabat and Mirza, and other learned natives; so that they now form an *Arabic School*, from which it is not pretended that there is any appeal in India.*

Mr. Martyn's own proper department is the Hindostanee language. Soon after his arrival, he translated the *Liturgy* of the church of England into that tongue; being the first who introduced the church service to our native subjects in Bengal. He found that many of the wives of the English soldiers were Hindostanee women, professing christianity, but who did not understand the English language, and being desirous to discharge faithfully the duties of his clerical office, he thought it proper to attempt such a translation. After reading prayers to the soldiers in English, he reads Hindostanee prayers to their wives, and to other natives. This original work, having received repeated revision and amendment, is esteemed by competent judges to be a perspicuous and faithful version of the sublime original. He also translated, about the same time, the parables and para-

* As Mr. Martyn and his associates at Cawnpore constitute the Arabic School in India, for the translation of the scriptures; so Dr. Carey, and the missionaries at Serampore, compose the Sanscrit School. See two memoirs lately published, and the proceedings of the Baptist Society, published annually.

bolic speeches, or apophthegms, of our Saviour, into the same language, with an explanation subjoined to each.

But the grand work which has chiefly engaged the attention of this oriental scholar, during the last four years, is his translation of the whole Bible into the HINDOSTANEE language. It has been often acknowledged, that a version of the scriptures into what is justly called "the grand popular language of Hindostan," would be the most generally useful in India. Mr. Martyn is in no haste to print any part of his work, being desirous that it should be first revised and approved by the best scholars. His chief difficulty is in settling the orthography of the language, and in ascertaining what proportion of words ought to be admitted from the Persian and Arabic fountains; for the Hindostanee is yet in its infancy, as a written and grammatical tongue; and it is probable, that Mr. Martyn's work will contribute much to fix its standard. To evince the care and accuracy which he proposes to himself in this translation, it will be proper to subjoin his last official report on the subject, dated December 1809.

"The Hindostanee New Testament has been finished some time, and submitted to the inspection of a variety of persons in different parts of the country; but the opinions formed of the work have not hitherto appeared to justify its publication. I am perfectly convinced of the inutility of attempting to please all; yet I thought it better to withhold from the press what longer experience, and the possession of more efficient instruments, might enable me to send forth, in a form more calculated to give general satisfaction. The person, whose assistance I was most anxious to obtain, has once more joined me; and I am now willing to hope that the word of God may be presented to the native of India, so as to be intelligible to the generality of readers.—The grammar of the language is nearly fixed by Mr. Gilchrist's learned and useful labours; but it is still difficult to write in it with a view to general utility; for the higher Mahomedans and men of learning will hardly peruse, with satisfaction, a book in which the *Persian* has not lent its aid to adorn the style. To the rest, a larger proportion of *Hindee* is more acceptable. The difficulty of ascertaining the point equally removed from either extreme, would be considerably lessened, were there any prose compositions in the language, of acknowledged purity. But unfortunately no such standard exists; no works of any description indeed have been found but poems. Lately some translations in Hindostanee prose have issued from the college of Fort-William; but as they have not yet stood the test of time, and are very little known in the country, they could not be safely referred to as a standard. Thus I have been left to the guidance of my own judgment far more than I could have wished."

In regard to the Arabic and Persian translations, both of which Mr. Martyn superintends, as well as the Hindostanee, he thus writes:—

"In the Persian and Arabic translations there are happily no such difficulties. The valuable qualities of our christian brother, Nathaniel Sabat, render this part of the work comparatively easy. As he is, I trust, a serious christian, the study of the word of God, and the translation of it, are of course a matter of choice with him, and a rigid adherence to the original a point of duty.* As a scholar his acquirements are very considerable. He was educated under the care of the most learned man in Bagdad: and, having continued to exercise himself in composition, he has acquired in consequence a critical acumen, and great command of words. His ill state of health renders it impossible to say exactly when the work he has undertaken will be finished; but if nothing untoward happen to interrupt us, you may expect the New Testament in the three languages, in the course of two years."

---

* The solicitude of these translators to infuse the true meaning of the original into their versions, and not to trust entirely to the English translation, will appear from the following observations of Mr. Martyn in his last letter.—"The Psalms we must leave till the end of the New Testament, for this solid reason, that I do not understand a considerable portion of that book. Much of the present translation is certainly unintelligible. It appears to me, that the two royal authors have suffered more from the plebeian touch of their interpreters, than even the prophets, or any others but Job. Hebrew has been of late my constant meditation."

THE JEWS.

There are three remarkable prophecies concerning the Jews.

1. "The children of Israel shall abide many days without a king, and without a prince, and without a sacrifice, and without an image, and without an ephod, and without teraphim." Hos. iii. 4.

2. "The Lord shall scatter thee among all people, from the one end of the earth even unto the other." Deut. xxviii. 64. And yet, "the people shall dwell alone, and shall not be reckoned amongst the nations." Num. xxiii. 9.

3. "Thou shalt become an astonishment, a proverb, and a bye-word among all the nations whither the Lord shall lead thee.—Among these nations shalt thou find no ease, neither shall the sole of thy foot have rest." Deut. xxviii. 37. 65.

The first of these prophecies is very remarkable; for who ever heard of a nation "abiding many days" without its civil and religious polity, and surviving its political existence? The very assertion seems to involve an absurdity. Did the Egyptians, Chaldeans, Greeks, or Romans, survive their civil and religious polity?

The second prediction is not less singular than the former; for if the Jews were to be received among the nations of the earth, why should they not "be reckoned with the nations?" Would any man, in a remote age, venture to foretel that there was a certain nation, which, in the ages to come, would be received and tolerated by all other nations, merely to be persecuted?*

But the third prophecy is such as must afford a contemplation to infidelity, to the end of time. The Jews

* To this day the Jews "are not reckoned" with the English nation. The prophetical record influenced the last parliamentary proceeding respecting them. In 1753, a bill was passed to naturalize the Jews; but after a few months it was repealed, the voice of the people demanded that the devoted nation should "not be reckoned with them." So true it is that our last national deliberation concerning this people was influenced by the ancient prophecy.—The time is now come when parliament may restore to the Jew the franchise of a fellow-creature, without contravening the divine decrees. It is prophesied again, that "Israel shall return to the Lord their God," and that the period of this event is not far remote. In obedience then to the dictate of this prophecy, let our christian nation proceed, without delay, to take away the reproach of the Jewish people; and announce the act in the most public and solemn manner, as an example to the rest of the world.

K

were to become "an astonishment, and a proverb, and a bye-word among all the nations," because they shed the blood of the Saviour of the world. Now it is not surprising that christians should reproach them for such a crime. But how should we expect that they would be "trodden down of the heathen world," who never heard of such a Saviour? Behold the Hindoo, at this day, punishing the Jew, without knowing the crime of which he has been guilty!

These three prophecies have been manifestly fulfilled; and if we had no other evidence, this is sufficient to prove "that there is a God, and that he hath made a revelation to man."

There is a fourth prophecy concerning this people, which will shortly be accomplished. The prophet Hosea, after foretelling that the children of Israel should abide many days without a king, adds these words:—"Afterwards shall they return, and seek the Lord their God, and David their king; and shall fear the Lord and his goodness in the latter days." Hosea iii. 5.

The question, which is now in the mouth of every christian, is that which was asked in the vision of the prophet Daniel on the same subject; "How long shall it be to the end of these wonders?" Dan. xii. 6. When shall the "indignation against the holy people be accomplished?" Dan. xi. 31. that they may "return and seek the Lord their God, and David their king?"

To Daniel the prophet, and to John the evangelist, was given a revelation of the great events of the general church to the end of time. Daniel foretels that the christian church shall be oppressed by the persecuting powers for "a time, times, and the dividing of a time." Dan. vii. 25. The same period he assigns for the accomplishment of the indignation against the holy people Israel. "One said, how long shall it be to the end of these wonders? And I heard the man clothed in linen, which was upon the waters of the river, when he held up his right hand and his left hand unto heaven, and sware by him that liveth for ever, that it shall be for a TIME, TIMES and a HALF; and when he shall have accomplished to scatter the power of the holy people, all these things shall be fulfilled." Dan. xii. 7. Now the same form of words is used in the Revelation of St. John, to express the duration of the Papal and Mahomedan powers. Oppressed by them, the church of Christ was to remain desolate in the wilderness, "for a TIME, TIMES, and HALF of a TIME." Rev. xii. 14. Every one, who is erudite in sacred prophecy, will understand that this great period of Daniel and St. John commences at the same era, namely, the rise of the persecuting powers; and that its duration is 1260 years.*

Here then are three great events hastening to their period; the extinction of the Papal dominion; the subversion of the Mahomedan power; and the accomplishment of the divine indignation against the holy people," or the return of the people of Israel "to seek the Lord their God, and David their king."

Our blessed Saviour has not left an event of this importance without notice. "The JEWS," saith he, "shall be led away captive into all nations; and Jerusalem shall be trodden down of the Gentiles, until the times of the Gentiles be fulfilled." Luke xxi. 24. What these "times of the Gentiles" are, our Lord has explained in his subsequent revelation to St. John. "The court which is without the temple is given unto the Gentiles; and the holy city shall they tread under foot FORTY and TWO MONTHS;" or, in prophetical language, at a day for a year, 1260 years. Rev. xi. 2.

The apostle Paul hath also recorded this event. "I would not, brethren, that ye should be ignorant of this mystery, that blindness, in part, is happened to ISRAEL, until the fulness of the Gentiles be come in; and so all Israel shall be saved." Rom. xi. 25. The fulness of time for the conversion of the Gentiles will be come in, when the Mahomedan and Papal obstructions are removed. Such events as the fall of the pope in the west, and of Mahomed in the east, both of whom persecuted the Jews to death, will probably be the means of awakening the Jews to consider the evidences of that religion which predicted the rise and fall of both.

But the grand prophecy of the apostle Paul on this subject, is that which respects the *consequence* of the conversion of the Jews. "The receiving of the Jews," saith he, "What shall it be to the world, but LIFE FROM THE DEAD?" Rom. xi. 15. Dispersed as they are in all

* See this period explained in p. 102.

countries, and speaking the languages of all countries, they will form a body of preachers ready prepared; and they need only say, "Behold the scriptures of God, in our possession; read our history there, as foretold three thousand years ago, and read the events in the annals of nations. We are witnesses to the world, and the world to us. Let the whole race of mankind unite and examine the fact."—"All ye inhabitants of the world, and dwellers on the earth, see ye, when the Lord lifteth up an ENSIGN on the mountains: and when he bloweth a TRUMPET, hear ye." Isaiah xviii. 3.—Thus will their preaching be to the world "LIFE from the DEAD."

But if the conversion of Israel is to take place when the Papal and Mahomedan powers have fallen, and who does not see that these events are near at hand? it might be expected that some signs of conciliation between Jews and Christians would now begin to be visible. And is not this the fact? Christians in all countries begin to consider, that "the indignation against the holy people" is nearly accomplished. Many events declare it. The indignation of man is relaxing. The prophecies have been fulfilled regarding it. The GREAT CRIME at CALVARY has been punished by all nations; and we now hear the words of the prophet addressing us, "Comfort ye, comfort ye my people, saith your God; speak ye comfortably to Jerusalem, and CRY unto her, that her warfare is accomplished, that her iniquity is pardoned." Isaiah xl. 1. This is the divine command; and behold, christians begin now, for the first time, "to speak comfortably to Jerusalem."

While the author was in the east, the state of the Jews, who are dispersed in different countries, frequently occupied his thoughts. He had heard that they existed in distinct colonies in certain parts of India; that some of them had arrived long before the christian era, and had remained in the midst of the Hindoos, to this time, a distinct and separate people, persecuted by the native princes, from age to age, and yet not destroyed; "burning, like the bush of Moses, and not consumed;" and he had a strong desire "to turn aside and see this great sight." His mind was impressed with the conviction that their preservation, in such a variety of regions, and under such a diversity of circumstances, could be only effected by the interposition of the divine PROVIDENCE, which reserved them, thus distinct, for some special and important purpose. And since the period of time for the accomplishment of this purpose was considered by many to be fast approaching, he wished to hear the sentiments of the Jews from their own lips, and to learn their actual impressions, as to their present circumstances and future hopes.

In his memorial respecting the Syrian christians, presented to Marquis Wellesley, the author also noticed the existence of an ancient colony of Jews on the coast of Malabar, particularly at Cochin; and as this place had recently become a part of the British empire, by conquest from the Dutch, Lord William Bentick, then governor of Madras, who had received letters from the supreme government, was pleased to direct the civil officer, who had charge of the department of Cochin,* to afford him every aid in the prosecution of his researches. His first tour to Cochin was in November 1806, and he remained in the country till February 1807. He again visited it in January 1808. He has only room, in this present work, to introduce a few notes from his Journal.

"*Cochin, Feb.* 4, 1807.

"I have been now in Cochin, or its vicinity, for upwards of two months, and have got well acquainted with the Jews. They do not live in the city of Cochin, but in a town about a mile distant from it, called Jews'-Town. It is almost wholly inhabited by the Jews, who have two respectable synagogues. Among them are some very intelligent men, who are not ignorant of the present history of nations. There are also Jews here from remote parts of Asia, so that this is the fountain of intelligence concerning that people in the east; there being constant communication by ships with the Red Sea, the Persian Gulf, and the mouths of the Indus. The resident Jews are divided into two classes, called

*Thomas Flower, Esq.

the Jerusalem or *White* Jews; and the Ancient or *Black* Jews. The White Jews reside at this place. The Black Jews have also a synagogue here; but the great body of that tribe inhabit towns in the interior of the province. I have now seen most of both classes. My inquiries referred chiefly to their antiquity, their manuscripts, and their sentiments concerning the present state of their nation."

THE JERUSALEM OR WHITE JEWS.

"ON my inquiry into the antiquity of the White Jews, they first delivered to me a narrative, in the Hebrew language, of their arrival in India, which has been handed down to them from their fathers; and then exhibited their ancient brass plate, containing their charter and freedom of residence, given by a king of Malabar. The following is the narrative of the events relating to their first arrival.

"'After the second temple was destroyed, (which may God speedily rebuild!) our fathers, dreading the conqueror's wrath, departed from Jerusalem, a numerous body of men, women, priests, and Levites, and came into this land. There were among them men of repute for learning and wisdom; and God gave the people favour in the sight of the king who at that time reigned here, and he granted them a place to dwell in, called *Cranganor*. He allowed them a patriarchal jurisdiction within the district, with certain privileges of nobility; and the royal grant was engraved, according to the custom of those days, on a plate of brass. This was done in the year from the creation of the world 4250 (A. D. 490); and this plate of brass we still have in possession. Our forefathers continued at Cranganor for about a thousand years, and the number of heads who governed were seventy-two. Soon after our settlement, other Jews followed us from Judea; and among these came that man of great wisdom, Rabbi Samuel, a Levite of Jerusalem, with his son, Rabbi Jehuda Levita. They brought with them the SILVER TRUMPETS, made use of at the time of the JUBILEE, which were saved when the second temple was destroyed; and we have heard from our fathers, that there were engraven upon those trumpets the letters of the ineffable Name.* There joined us also from *Spain*, and other places, from time to time, certain tribes of Jews, who had heard of our prosperity. But at last, discord arising among ourselves, one of our chiefs called to his assistance an Indian king, who came upon us with a great army, destroyed our houses, palaces, and strong holds, dispossessed us of Cranganor, killed part of us, and carried part into captivity. By these massacres we were reduced to a small number. Some of the exiles came and dwelt at Cochin, where we have remained ever since, suffering great changes from time to time. There are amongst us some of the children of Israel (Beni-Israel) who came from the country of Ashkenaz, from Egypt, from Tsoba, and other places, besides those who formerly inhabited this country.'

"The native annals of Malabar confirm the foregoing account, in the principal circumstances, as do the Mahomedan histories of the later ages; for the Mahomedans have been settled here in great numbers since the eighth century.

"The desolation of Cranganor the Jews describe as being like the desolation of Jerusalem in miniature. They were first received into the country with some favour and confidence, agreeably to the tenor of the general prophecy concerning the Jews; for no country was to reject them: and after they had obtained some wealth, and attracted the notice of men, they are precipitated to the lowest abyss of human suffering and reproach. The recital of the sufferings of the Jews at Cranganor resembles much that of the Jews at Jerusalem, as given by Josephus.

"I now requested they would show me their brass plate. Having been given by a native king, it is written, of course, in the *Malabaric* language and character; and is now so old that it cannot be well understood. The Jews preserve a Hebrew translation of it, which they presented to me; but the Hebrew itself is very difficult,

* This circumstance of the jubilee trumpets is to be found in a similar account of the Jews of Malabar, published in the "History of the Works of the Learned," for March 1699. It is not necessary to suppose that these trumpets belonged to the temple; for it is well known, that in every considerable town in Judea there were jubilee trumpets.

and they do not agree among themselves, as to the meaning of some words. I have employed, by their permission, an engraver at Cochin, to execute a fac-simile of the original plate, on copper.* This ancient document begins in the following manner, according to the Hebrew translation: †

"'In the peace of God, the King, which hath made the earth, according to his pleasure. To this God, I, AIRVI BRAHMIN, have lifted up my hand, and have granted by this deed, which many hundred thousand years shall run———I, dwelling in Cranganor, have granted, in the thirty-sixth year of my reign, in the strength of power I have granted, in the strength of power I have given in inheritance, to JOSEPH RABBAN.'

"Then follow the privileges of nobility; such as permission to ride on the elephant; to have a herald to go before, to announce the name and dignity; to have the lamp of the day; to walk on carpets spread upon the earth; and to have trumpets and cymbals sounded before him. King Airvi then appoints Joseph Rabban to be 'chief and governor of the houses of congregation (the synagogues), and of certain districts, and of the sojourners in them.' What proves the importance of the Jews at the period when this grant was made, is, that it is signed by seven kings as witnesses. 'And to this are witnesses, king Bivada Cubertin Mitadin, and he is king of *Travancore*. King Airla Nada Mana Vikriin, and he is the *Samorin*. King Veloda Nada Archarin Shatin, and he is king of *Argot*.' The remaining four kings are those of *Palgatchery, Colastri, Carbinath,* and *Vara-changur*. There is no date in this document, further than what may be collected from the reign of the prince, and the names of the royal witnesses. Dates are not usual in old Malabaric writings. One fact is evident, that the Jews must have existed a considerable time in the country, before they could have obtained such a grant. The tradition before mentioned

* The original is engraved on both sides of the plate, the fac-simile forms two plates. These are now deposited in the public library at the university of Cambridge.

† A copy of this Hebrew translation was sent to the university with the other MSS.—I have a copy in my possession.

assigns for the date of the transaction, the year of the creation 4250, which is, in Jewish computation, A. D. 490. It is well known, that the famous Malabaric king, Ceram Perumal, made grants to the Jews, Christians, and Mahomedans, during his reign; but that prince flourished in the eighth or ninth century."

THE BLACK JEWS.

"It is only necessary to look at the countenance of the Black Jews to be satisfied that their ancestors must have arrived in India many ages before the White Jews. Their Hindoo complexion, and their very imperfect resemblance to the European Jews, indicate that they have been detached from the parent stock in Judea many ages before the Jews in the west; and that there have been intermarriages with families not Israelitish. I had heard that those tribes, which had passed the Indus, have assimilated so much to the customs and habits of the countries in which they live, that they may be sometimes seen by a traveller, without being recognised as Jews. In the interior towns of Malabar, I was not always able to distinguish the Jew from the Hindoo. I hence perceived how easy it may be to mistake the tribes of Jewish descent among the Afghans and other nations in the northern parts of Hindostan. The White Jews look upon the Black Jews as an inferior race, and as not of a *pure* cast; which plainly demonstrates that they do not spring from a common stock in India.

"The Black Jews communicated to me much interesting intelligence concerning their brethren the ancient Israelites in the east; traditional indeed in its nature, but in general illustrative of true history. They recounted the names of many other small colonies resident in northern India, Tartary and China; and gave me a written list of sixty-five places. I conversed with those who had lately visited many of these stations, and were about to return again. The Jews have a never-ceasing communication with each other in the east. Their families indeed are generally stationary, being subject to despotic princes; but the men move much about in a commercial capacity; and the same individual will pass through many extensive countries. So that when any thing interesting to the nation of the Jews takes place, the rumour will pass rapidly throughout all Asia.

"I inquired concerning their brethren, the Ten Tribes. They said that it was commonly believed among them, that the great body of the Israelites are to be found in Chaldea, and in the countries contiguous to it, being the very places whither they were first carried into captivity; that some few families had migrated into regions more remote, as to Cochin and Rajapoor in India, and to other places yet farther to the east; but that the bulk of the nation, though now much reduced in number, had not to this day removed two thousand miles from *Samaria*.—Among the Black Jews I could not find many copies of the Bible. They informed me, that in certain places of the remote dispersion, their brethren have but some small portions of the scriptures, and that the *prophetical* books were rare; but that they themselves, from their vicinity to the White Jews, have been supplied, from time to time, with the whole of the Old Testament.

"From these communications I plainly perceive the important duty which now devolves on christians possessing the art of *printing*, to send to the Jews in the east, copies of the Hebrew scriptures, and particularly of the *prophetical* books. If only the prophecies of *Isaiah* and *Daniel* were published among them, the effect might be great. They do not want the law so much. But the prophetical books would appear among them with some novelty, particularly in a detached form; and could be easily circulated through the remotest parts of Asia."

MANUSCRIPTS.

"Almost in every house I find Hebrew books, printed or manuscript; particularly among the White Jews. Most of the printed Hebrew of Europe has found its way to Cochin, through the medium of the Portuguese and Dutch commerce of former times. When I questioned the Jews concerning the old copies of the scriptures, which had been read in the synagogues from age to age; some told me that it was usual to *bury* them, when decayed by time and use. Others said that this was not always the case. I despaired at first of being able to procure any of the old biblical writings; but after I had been in the country about six weeks, and they found that I did not expect to obtain them merely as presents, some copies were *recovered*. The White Jews had only the Bible written on parchment, and of modern appearance, in their synagogue; but I was informed that the Black Jews possessed formerly copies written on *goat-skins;* and that in the synagogue of the Black Jews there was an old record chest, into which the decayed copies of their scriptures had been thrown. I accordingly went to the synagogue with a few of the chief men, and examined the contents, which some of them said they had never looked at before, and did not seem greatly to value. The manuscripts were of various kinds, on parchment, goat-skins, and cotton paper. I negociated for them hastily, and wrapped them up in two cloths, and gave them to the Jews to carry home to my house. I had observed some murmuring amongst the bystanders in the synagogue, while I was examining the chest; and before we appeared in the streets, the alarm had gone forth, that the christians were robbing the synagogue of the law. There were evident symptoms of tumult, and the women and children collected and were following us. I requested some of the more respectable Jews to accompany me out of the town; but I had scarcely arrived at my own house at Cochin, when the persons who had permitted me to take the manuscripts, came in evident agitation, and told me I must restore them immediately to calm the popular rage. Others had gone to complain to the chief magistrate, Thomas Flower, esq. And now I had lost my spoil, but for the friendly counsel and judicious conduct of Mr. Flower. He directed that all the manuscripts should be delivered up to him, and that there should be no further proceedings on the subject without his authority. To this the Jews agreed. There was some plea of justice on my side, as it was understood that I had given a valuable consideration. In the mean time he allowed a few days to pass, that the minds of the people might become tranquil, and he then summoned some of the more liberal men, and gave them a hearing on the subject. In the mean time I thought it prudent to retire from Cochin, for a day or two, and went to Cranganor, about sixteen miles off, to Colonel Macaulay, the British resident at Travancore, who was then at the house of Mr. Drummond, the collector of Malabar. On my return to Cochin, Mr. Flower informed me that all the manuscripts were to be returned to my house; that I was to select what was *old*, and of little use to the Jews, and to give back to them what was *new*. The affair ended however in the Jews permitting me generously to retain some part of the *new*.

"I have since made a tour through the towns of the Black Jews in the interior of the country, *Tritoor*, *Paroor*, *Chenotta* and *Maleh*. I have procured a good many manuscripts, chiefly in the rabbinical character, some of which the Jews themselves cannot read; and I do not know what to say to their traditions. A copy of the scriptures belonging to Jews of the east, who might be supposed to have had no communication with Jews in the west, has been long considered a desideratum in Europe; for the western Jews have been accused by some learned men of altering or omitting certain words in the Hebrew text, to invalidate the argument of christians. But Jews in the east, remote from the controversy, would have no motive for such corruptions. One or two of the MSS. which I have just procured, will probably be of some service in this respect. One of them is an old copy of the Books of Moses, written on a roll of leather. The skins are sewed together, and the roll is about forty-eight feet in length. It is, in some places, worn out, and the holes have been sewed up with pieces of parchment. Some of the Jews suppose that this roll came originally from Senna in Arabia; others have heard that it was brought from Cashmir. The Cabul Jews, who travel into the interior of China, say that in some synagogues the law is still written on a roll of leather, made of goats' skins dyed red; not on vellum, but on a soft flexible leather; which agrees with the description of the roll above mentioned.*

* Mr. Yeates, formerly of All Souls College, Oxford, and editor of the Hebrew grammar, has been employed for the last two years at Cambridge, in arranging and collating the Hebrew and Syriac MSS. brought from India. His collation of the roll of the Pentateuch above mentioned, is now finished,

"Ever since I came among these people, and heard their sentiments on the prophecies, and their confident hopes of returning to *Jerusalem*, I have thought much on the means of obtaining a version of the NEW TESTAMENT in the Hebrew language, and circulating it among them and their brethren in the east. I had heard that there were one or two translations of the Testament in their own possession, but they were studiously kept out of my sight, for a considerable time. At last however they were produced by individuals in a private manner. One of them is written in the small rabbinical or Jerusalem character; the other in a large square letter. The history of the former is very interesting. The translator, a learned rabbi, conceived the design of making an accurate version of the New Testament, for the express purpose of *confuting* it. His style is copious and elegant, like that of a master in the language, and the translation is in general faithful. It does not indeed appear that he wished to pervert the meaning of a single sentence; but depending on his own abilities and renown as a scholar, he hoped to be able to controvert its doctrines, and to triumph over it by fair contest in the presence of the world. There is yet a mystery about the circumstances of this man's death, which time will perhaps unfold: the Jews are not inclined to say much to me about him. His version is complete, and written with greater freedom and ease towards the end than at the beginning. How astonishing it is that an enemy should have done this! that he should have persevered resolutely and calmly to the end of his work! not indeed always *calmly;* for there is sometimes a note of execration on the Sacred Person who is the subject of it, to unburden his mind and ease the conflict of his labouring soul. At the close of the Gospels, as if afraid of the converting power of his own translation, 'he calls heaven to witness that he had undertaken the work with the professed design of opposing the *Epicureans;*' by which term he contemptuously means the christians.

"I have had many interesting conferences with the

and will form a volume in quarto. The university has, with great liberality, resolved that this book shall be printed at the expense of the university, for the benefit of Mr. Yeates; and Dr. Marsh, the learned editor of Michaelis, has written a note on the antiquity and importance of the manuscript, which will form a preface to the work.

Jews, on the subject of their present state; and have been much struck with two circumstances; their constant reference to the DESOLATION of Jerusalem, and their confident hope that it will be one day REBUILT. The desolation of the holy city is ever present to the minds of the Jews, when the subject is concerning themselves as a *nation;* for, though without a king and without a country, they constantly speak of the *unity* of their nation. Distance of time and place seems to have no effect in obliterating the remembrance of the Desolation. I often thought of the verse in the Psalms, 'If I forget thee, O Jerusalem, let my right hand forget her cunning.' They speak of Palestine as being close at hand, and easily accessible. It is become an ordinance of their rabbins in some places, that when a man builds a new house, he shall leave a small part of it unfinished, as an emblem of ruin, and write on it these words, *Zecher Lachorchan,* i. e. In MEMORY of the DESOLATION.

"Their hopes of REBUILDING the walls of Jerusalem, the THIRD and LAST time, under the auspices of the Messiah, or of a second Cyrus, before his coming, are always expressed with great confidence. They have a general impression, that the period of their liberation from the heathen is not very remote; and they consider the present commotions in the earth as gradually loosening their bonds. 'It is,' say they, 'a sure sign of our approaching restoration, that in almost all countries there is a GENERAL RELAXATION of the persecution against us.' I pressed strongly upon them the prophecies of Daniel. In former times that prophet was not in repute among the Jews, because he predicted the coming of the Messiah at the end of 'the seventy weeks;' and his book has been actually removed from the list of prophetic writings, and remains, to this day, among the *Hagiographa,* such as Job, the Psalms, the Proverbs, Ruth; but he now begins to be popular among those who have studied him, because he has predicted that the final 'accomplishment of the indignation against the holy people' is near at hand. The strongest argument to press upon the mind of a Jew, at this period, is to explain to his conviction Daniel's period of 1260 years; and then to show the analogy which it bears to the period of the evangelist John, concerning the Papal and Mahomedan powers; with the state of which the Jews are well acquainted.

"I passed through the burial-ground of the Jews the other day. Some of the tombs are handsomely constructed, and have Hebrew inscriptions, in prose and verse. This mansion of the dead is called by the Jews *Beth Haiim*, or 'The House of the Living.'

"Being much gratified with my visit to the Jews of Malabar, and desirous to maintain some communication with them, I have engaged a very respectable member of their community to accompany me with his servant to Bengal, and to remain with me in the capacity of Hebrew *Moonshee*, or teacher, until my return to England. Observing that in the houses of the White Jews there are many volumes of printed Hebrew, mostly of the fifteenth and sixteenth centuries, which are rarely met with in England, I have employed *Misrahi*, that is the name of my Moonshee, to collect some of the most valuable."

At the beginning of the following year (1808) the author visited Cochin a second time, and proceeded afterwards to Bombay, where he had an opportunity of meeting with some very intelligent men of the Jewish nation. They had heard of his conferences with the Cochin Jews, and were desirous to discuss certain topics, particularly the prophecies of Isaiah; and they engaged in them with far more spirit and frankness, he thought, than their brethren at Cochin had done. They told him, that if he would take a walk to the bazaar in the suburb, without the walls of Bombay town, he would find a synagogue without a *Sepher Tora*, or book of the law. He did so, and found it to be the case. The minister and a few of the Jews assembled, and showed him their synagogue, in which there were some loose leaves of prayers in manuscript, but no book of the law. The author did not understand that they disapproved of the law; but they had no copy of it. They seemed to have little knowledge of the Jewish scriptures or history. This only proved what he had been often told, that small portions of the Jewish nation melt away from time to time, and are absorbed in the mass of the heathen world.

Nor is this any argument against the truth of the prophecy, which declares that they should remain a separate and distinct people; for these are mere *exceptions.* Conversions to christianity in the early ages would equally militate against the prediction, taken in an absolute sense.

THE TEN TRIBES.

The tribes of Israel are no longer to be inquired after by name. The purpose, for which they were once divided into tribes, was accomplished when the genealogy of the Messiah was traced to the stem of David. Neither do the Israelites themselves know certainly from what families they are descended. And this is a chief argument against the Jews, to which the author never heard that a Jew could make a sensible reply. The tribe of *Judah* was selected as that from which the Messiah should come; and behold, the Jews do not know which of them are of the tribe of Judah.

While the author was amongst the Jews of Malabar, he made frequent inquiries concerning the Ten Tribes. When he mentioned that it was the opinion of some, that they had migrated from the Chaldean provinces, he was asked to what country we supposed they had gone, and whether we had ever heard of their moving in a great army on such an expedition. It will be easy perhaps to show, that the great body of the Ten Tribes remain to this day in the countries to which they were first carried captive. If we can discover where they were in the first century of the christian era, which was seven hundred years after the carrying away to Babylon, and again where they were in the fifth century, we certainly may be able to trace them up to this time.

Josephus, who wrote in the reign of Vespasian, recites a speech made by king Agrippa to the Jews, wherein he exhorts them to submit to the Romans, and expostulates with them in these words:—"What, do you stretch your hopes beyond the river Euphrates? Do any of you think that your fellow-tribes will come to your aid out of *Adiabene?* Besides, if they would come, the Parthian will not permit it." (*Jos. de Bell.* Lib. ii. c. 28.) We learn from this oration, delivered to the Jews themselves, and by a king of the Jews, that the Ten Tribes were then captive in Media under the Persian princes.

In the fifth century, Jerome, author of the Vulgate, treating of the dispersed Jews, in his notes upon Hosea, has these words: "Unto this day, the Ten Tribes are subject to the kings of the Persians, nor has their captivity ever been loosed." (Tom. vi. p. 7.) And again he says, "The Ten Tribes inhabit at this day the cities and mountains of the Medes." (Tom. vi. p. 80.)

There is no room left for doubt on this subject. Have we heard of any expedition of the Jews "going forth from that country, since that period, like the Goths and Huns, to conquer nations?" Have we ever heard of their rising in insurrection to burst the bands of their captivity? To this day, both Jews and Christians are generally in a state of captivity in these despotic countries. No family dares to leave the kingdom without permission of the king.*

Mahomedanism reduced the number of the Jews exceedingly; it was presented to them at the point of the sword. We know that multitudes of christians received it; for example, "the seven churches of Asia;" and we may believe, that an equal proportion of Jews were proselyted by the same means. In the provinces of Cashmire and Affghanistan, some of the Jews submitted to great sacrifices, and they remain Jews to this day; but the greater number yielded, in the course of ages, to the power of the reigning religion. Their countenance, their language, their names, their rites and observances, and their history, all conspire to establish the fact.† We may judge, in some degree, of the number of those who would yield to the sword of Mahomed, and conform, in appearance at least, to what was called a *sister religion*, from the number of those who conformed to the christian religion, under the influence of the inquisition

* Joseph Emin, a christian well known in Calcutta, wished to bring his family from Ispahan; but he could not effect it, though our government interested itself in his behalf.

† Mr. Forster was so much struck with the general appearance, garb and manners of the Cashmirians, as to think, without any previous knowledge of the fact, that he had been suddenly transported among a nation of JEWS. See Forster's travels.

in Spain and Portugal. Orobio, who was himself a Jew, states in his history, that there were upwards of twenty thousand Jews in Spain alone, who, from fear of the inquisition, professed christianity, some of whom were priests and bishops. The tribes of the Affghan race are very numerous, and of different casts; and it is probable, that the proportion which is of Jewish descent is not great. The Affghan nations extend on both sides of the Indus, and inhabit the mountainous region, commencing in western Persia. They differ in language, customs, religion, and countenançe, and have little knowledge of each other. Some tribes have the countenance of the Persian, and some of the Hindoo; and some tribes are evidently of Jewish extraction.

Calculating then the number of Jews, who now inhabit the provinces of ancient Chaldea, or the contiguous countries, and who still profess Judaism; and the number of those who embraced Mahomedanism, or some form of it, in the same regions; we may be satisfied, "That the greater part of the Ten Tribes, which *now exist*, are to be found in the countries of their first captivity."

RESTORATION OF THE JEWS.

THAT many of the Jews, when liberated from their state of oppression, will return to Judea, appears probable from the general tenor of prophecy, and from their own natural and unconquerable attachment to that country; but we know not for what purpose they should *all* return thither; and it is perfectly unnęcessary to contend for the fact, or to impose it as a tenet of faith. We perceive no reason why they should leave the nations in which they live, when these nations are no longer *heathen*. Nor is it possible, in numerous cases, to ascertain who are Jews and who are not. It is also true, that before Judea could nourish the whole body of Jews, even in their present reduced state, the ancient FERTILITY, which was taken away according to prophecy (Deut. xxviii. 23 and 38), must be restored by miracle. But we have no warrant to look for a miracle under the finished dispensation of the gospel. We possess "the MORE sure word of prophecy," (2 Pet. i. 19), and look not for signs and wonders. We expect no miracle for the Jews, but that of their conversion to christianity; which will be a greater miracle, than if the first temple were to rise in its gold and costly stones, and Solomon were again to reign over them in all his glory.

Much caution is also required in stating to them our opinions concerning the MILLENNIUM, or period of universal truth and felicity. It was prophesied to Israel, about seven hundred years before the coming of the Messiah, that a time should be, "when nation should no longer lift the sword against nation, neither should men learn war any more:" when "the knowledge of the Lord," which was then confined to Judea, "should cover the earth as the waters cover the sea;" and when "they should not teach every man his neighbour, saying, Know the Lord, for ALL should know him from the least to the greatest." These prophecies were fulfilled generally when the Messiah appeared. The gospel of peace was preached to men, and "the sound thereof went to the ends of the earth." The last prediction, which is the clearest and strongest of all, "They shall not teach every man his neighbour, saying, Know the Lord, for ALL shall know him, from the least to the greatest," is expressly quoted by the apostle Paul (Heb. viii. 11.) as having been already fulfilled by the manifestation of Christ, who abrogated the old covenant with Israel, which was confined to FEW, and made a new covenant with the world, which was extended to ALL.

It is believed, however, that the predictions above recited will receive a more particular accomplishment hereafter, and that the glory even of the primitive church shall be far surpassed. But it does not appear, that the conversion of men at any future period will be UNIVERSAL. It is evident indeed, from the sure word of prophecy, that there will be a long time of *general* holiness and peace, which will succeed to the present reign of vice and misery, probably "a thousand years;" during which, righteousness will be as common as wickedness is now; and further, that this period is *at hand, even at the door*.* But I see no ground for be-

* See Scott's Bible, Rev. xx. 4.

lieving that such righteousness will be universal, or that this life will ever be other than a state of probation and trial to qualify for "meetness for the heavenly kingdom." Our Saviour sets forth, in different places, the character of his church, to the end of time, and that character is always the *same*. The gospel he compares to "seed sown by the sower, some on *good* and some on *bad* ground." Those who hear this gospel he compares to men building on the *rock*, or on the *sand*; travelling in the *broad*, or in the *narrow* way; and to *wheat* and *tares* growing in the same field. "The field is the world," saith our Lord; "the good seed are the children of the kingdom: the tares are the children of the wicked one: the enemy that sowed them is the devil: the harvest is the end of the world; and the reapers are the angels." (Matth. xiii. 39.) This we believe to be a picture of the visible church to the end of time.

In regard to the progress, conflict, and final extent of the gospel, our Saviour notices all these circumstances generally in his last discourse to his disciples. In the twenty-fourth chapter of St. Matthew, he gives an epitome of his more detailed prophecy in the Book of Revelation. He foretels that there shall be "wars and rumours of wars, persecutions, famines, pestilences, earthquakes, false prophets and apostasies:" and then he adds, "And this gospel of the kingdom shall be preached in all the world for a WITNESS unto all nations: and then shall the end come."

To suppose that there will be a period when the church on earth shall be no longer militant, is to suppose that a time will come when the christian may die without being able to say, "I have fought a good fight;" when there will be little inward corruption, and little outward opposition; little vestige of the old Adam, in the new race, and little use for the old Bible, in the new state of things. Let us interpret scripture soberly. When the millennium arrives, knowledge and holiness will be general; but not universal. Perfection is to be attained not in this world, but in heaven.

ON the author's return to England, he found that a society had been instituted for the conversion of the Jews; and he was not a little surprised to hear that some christians had opposed its institution. He was less surprised at this, however, when he was informed that objections had been brought against the society for the circulation of the BIBLE. It is possible to urge political arguments against christianity itself. Such a spirit as this does not seem entitled to much courtesy; for it springs directly from this assumption, That the Bible is not from God, or, That there is something greater than TRUTH.

The grand object, which now engages the attention of the Jewish institution, is a translation of the New Testament into the Hebrew language. To assist them in this important work, a copy of the manuscript found in Malabar, now commonly called the *Travancore Testament*, has been presented to them.* The volume has been fairly transcribed by Mr. Yeates, of Cambridge, in the square Hebrew character, and forms three volumes, quarto. The question now under consideration by the society is, whether it shall be received as the *basis* for the general translation. The first sheet of the intended version has already been printed off, for the purpose of being submitted as a specimen to the best Hebrew scholars in the kingdom, both Jews and Christians; in order that it may go forth in as perfect a form as may be. So that it is possible, that before the end of the present year, the Four Gospels will be published, and copies sent to the Jews in the east, as the FIRST-FRUITS of the Jewish institution. It is very remarkable, that this should be the very year which was calculated long ago, by a learned man, as that in which "the times of happiness to Israel" should begin. In the year 1677, Mr. Samuel Lee, a scholar of enlarged views, who had studied the prophetical writings with great attention, published a small volume, entitled, "Israel Redux, or The Restauration of Israel." He calculates the event from the prophecies of Daniel and of St. John, and commences the great period of 1260 years, not from A. D. 608, which we think correct, but from A. D. 476, which brings it to 1736. He then adds, "After the great conflicts with the Papal powers in the west, will begin the stirs and commotions about the Jews and Israel in the east. If then to 1736 we add 30 more,

* See p. 73.

they reach to 1766; but the times of perplexity are determined (by Daniel) to last 45 years longer. If then we conjoin those 45 years more to 1766, it produces one thousand eight hundred and ELEVEN, for those times of happiness to Israel."*

VERSIONS OF THE SCRIPTURES FOR THE JEWS,

IN THE ORIENTAL LANGUAGES.

SINCE writing the above, the author has received the following communication from the Rev. David Brown, dated Calcutta, March 15, 1810:—

"Dr. Leyden, of the college of Fort-William, in a letter communicated to me yesterday, has offered to conduct translations of the scriptures in the following languages; viz.

1. AFFGHAN,
2. CASHMIRIAN,
3. JAGHATAI,
4. SIAMESE,
5. BUGIS,
6. MACASSAR, AND
7. MALDIVIAN.

"The Jaghatai is the original Turcoman language, as spoken in the central districts of Asia. The Bugis is the language of the Celebes. The Macassar is spoken at Macassar, in the Celebes, and in the great island of BORNEO.

"Dr. Leyden is assisted, as you know, by learned natives in the compilation of grammars and vocabularies in the above languages, and entertains no doubt that he shall be able to effect correct versions of the scriptures in them all."

Thus, sooner than could have been expected, we are likely to have the Bible translated into the language of the CELEBES.† But who can estimate the importance of a translation of the scriptures into the languages of Affghana and Cashmire, those Jewish regions!

The Jaghatai or *Zagathai*, is the language of Great Bucharia, which was called Zagathai, from a son of

* See "Israel Redux;" page 122, printed in Cornhill, London, 1677.

† See p. 51 for an account of the importance of this language.

Zenghis Khan. It is an auspicious circumstance for Dr. Leyden's translation of the Jaghatai, that Prince Zagathai himself embraced christianity, and made a public profession of the gospel in his capital of Samarchand.* There were at that period above a hundred christian churches in the province; and some of them remain to this day. We are also informed, both by the Nestorian and Romish writers, that there was a version of the New Testament and Psalms in a *Tartar* language. Dr. Leyden will soon discover whether this was the Jaghatai. That language is spoken in Bochara, Balk and Samarchand, and in other cities of Usbeck, and Independent Tartary. This is the country which Dr. Giles Fletcher, who was envoy of queen Elizabeth, at the court of the czar of Muscovy, has assigned as the principal residence of the decendants of the *Ten Tribes*. He argues from their *place*, from the name of their cities, from their *language*, which contains Hebrew and Chaldaic words, and from their peculiar *rites*, which are Jewish. Their principal city Samarchand is pronounced *Samarchian*, which Dr. Fletcher thinks might be a name given by the Israelites after their own *Samaria* in Palestine. (See Israel Redux, p. 12.) Benjamin of Tudela, who travelled into this country, in the twelfth century, and afterwards published his *Itinerary*, says, "In Samarchand, the city of Tamerlane, there are 50,000 Jews under the presidency of Rabbi Obadiah; and in the mountains and cities of Nisbor, there are four tribes of Israel resident, viz. Dan, Zabulon, Asher, and Napththali."† It is remarkable that the people of Zagathai should be constantly called Ephthalites and *Nephthalites* by the Byzantine writers, who alone had any information concerning them.‡ The fact seems to be, that, if from Babylon as a centre, you describe a segment of a circle, from the northern shore of the Caspian Sea to the heads of the Indus, you will enclose the territories containing the chief body of the dispersed tribes of Israel.

This design of Dr. Leyden to superintend the translation of the scriptures in SEVEN new languages marks the liberal views and the enterprising and ardent mind of that scholar, and will be hailed by the friends of christi-

* See Mosheim's Eccl. Tartar History, p. 40.

† See Benjamini Itinerarium, p. 97.

‡ Theophanes, p. 79.

anity in Europe as a noble undertaking, deserving their utmost eulogy and patronage. It will give pleasure to all those who have hitherto taken any interest in "the restoration of learning in the east," to see that the college of Fort-William is producing such excellent fruit. May its fame be perpetual!*

THE BIBLIOTHECA BIBLICA IN BENGAL.

THE Bibliotheca Biblica is a repository for Bibles in the Oriental languages, and for Bibles only. They are here deposited for sale, at moderate prices; and lists of the various versions are sent to remote parts of Asia, that individuals may know where to purchase them; the commerce from the port of Calcutta rendering the transmission of books extremely easy. Those who desire to have copies for gratuitous distribution are supplied at the cost prices. This institution is under the immediate superintendence of the Rev. David Brown, late provost of the college of Fort-William, who was himself the founder; and it is supported by all the translators of the Bible in India, who send in their versions, and by the college of Fort-William, which sends in its versions.

There have been already deposited in the Bibliotheca Biblica four thousand volumes, in the following languages:

ARABIC,	ORISSA,
PERSIAN,	BENGALEE,
HINDOSTANEE,	CHINESE,
SANSCRIT,	PORTUGUESE, AND
MAHRATTA,	ENGLISH.

* There are now several Orientalists, members of the Asiatic Society, who have been engaged in translating the Holy Scriptures. We hope hereafter to see the name of Mr. Colebrooke added to the number. Mr. C. is the father of Sanscrit literature, and has lately published an Essay on the Sanscrit Poetry and Metres. How much gratified should we be to see a version of the Pentateuch from his pen! or at least a critique on the New Testament, which has been already translated into Sanscrit. Mr. C. is the proper man to oppose the Pentateuch to the Hindoo Cosmogony, and to invite the Brahmins to contemplate the Mosaic records, in classical Sanscrit. This would be a work worthy of his great erudition; and his name, as a Sanscrit scholar, would then, indeed, live for ever. Mr. Colebrooke has ever shown kindness to the humble misionaries, who have been cultivating the Sanscrit tongue; he has supplied them with books, and afforded them every liberal aid; it will give him no regret, at his last hour, to think that he has had it in his power, in any degree, to promote the cause of christianity.

These traslations have been chiefly furnished by the following persons: —

Dr. William Carey and Mr. Joshua Marshman; two men, whose names will probably go down to the latest posterity in India, as faithful translators of the holy scriptures. These have furnished the *Sanscrit*, *Bengalee*, *Orissa* and *Mahratta*.

Nathaniel Sabat, from Arabia, has contributed the *Persian*. The first Persian translation (which is also in the Bibliotheca) was made by the late Lieutenant-Col. Colebrooke, surveyor-general in Bengal; and it "blesses his memory."

Mirza Filrut furnishes the *Hindostanee*. There is another Hindostanee translation by the missionaries at Serampore; and

Mr. Joannes Lassar is author of the *Chinese*.

There will be a large accession to this honourable catalogue in a year or two. It is astonishing how much this simple institution, like the Bible society in England, has attracted the attention of the public, native and European, wherever it has been announced. The superintendents have recently sent to England for the following supply of Bibles, which is now collecting for them, viz.

	Old & New Test.	New Test.
English	2000	2000
Portuguese . . .	2000	2000
French	500	500
German	500	
Dutch	500	
Danish	500	
Spanish	200	
Latin	100	100
Italian	100	100
Hebrew	100	
Greek	100	100
Syriac	—	100
Swedish	50	
Prussian	50	
Russian	50	

Armenian, Malay and Arabic, as many copies as can be procured.

Attached to the Bibliotheca Biblica is a Translation

LIBRARY, containing books for the use of the translators of the scriptures. As this library is not complete, many of the necessary works not being procurable in India, a list of the volumes required will be published; in the hope that learned bodies and individuals having duplicates, will be pleased to present them to the Bibliotheca Biblica in Bengal.

This institution was first organized by the Rev. Mr. Brown, with a full reliance on the patronage of the British and Foreign Bible Society, which has cordially embraced his views, and of the Society for promoting Christian Knowledge, and of the Universities in the United Kingdom, which we hope will enrich its translation library.

The Rev. David Brown, senior chaplain of the East India Company in Bengal, formerly of Magdalen College, Cambridge, has now been twenty-seven years resident in India; and is the zealous promoter of sacred learning in the east. He is educating his THREE SONS in India, solely with the view of qualifying them for the important purpose of extending the knowledge of christianity in Asia. Being himself a Hebrew scholar, his first object has been to ground them well in the *Hebrew* and *Syriac* languages; rightly judging that a knowledge of these, forms the best foundation for ability to produce accurate translations of the scriptures in the other oriental tongues. But they have now added to these first languages the *Arabic*, *Persian*, and *Hindostanee*, which they pronounce like natives of the east. They have had the advantage of the best teachers in the different languages, particularly of SHALOM, an eminent Hebrew scholar from Arabia. So that this little institution in Mr. Brown's house, may be called the HEBREW SCHOOL in Bengal.

It is understood to be Mr. Brown's intention to send his three sons to England, at the proper age, to finish their education at the university, and to enter the church; with the view of their returning to exercise their ministrations in India. Mr. Brown himself has now seen two or three generations pass away in Calcutta; how short is a Calcutta generation! and has exhibited to a large and refined society the doctrine and the example of a faithful minister of the gospel. Marquis Cornwallis first recommended him to the court of directors as a proper person to fill his present important situation, and this he did from a personal knowledge of his truly upright and disinterested character. In the many governments which have succeeded, there is not one, as the author believes, which has not recorded a public testimony to the merits of their senior chaplain. Marquis Wellesley, in particular, honoured him with his confidence and esteem, to the end of his administration. It was under the auspices of that nobleman, that Mr. Brown instituted the "Calcutta CHARITABLE FUND for distressed Europeans and others;" of which it may be truly said, that it has been a fountain of mercy to thousands in Bengal for ten years past, it having been established in the first year of the new century.* Mr. Brown would have probably returned from India with his large family by this time, but his diffusive benevolence in private charity, and in public undertakings, both in India and in England, and the frequent demands on a man in his public station, he being at the head of the church in Bengal, have not permitted him to increase his fortune suitably. And now, the prospect which opens to his view of being more extensively useful than before, in encouraging translations of the scriptures, in promoting the objects of the Bible society, and in educating his sons for the oriental church, makes him willing to remain a few years longer in India.

THE ARMENIANS.

A LEARNED author, in a work published about the beginning of last century, entitled "The Light of the Gospel, rising on all nations," observes, "that the Armenian christians will be most eminently qualified for the office of extending the knowledge of christianity throughout the nations of Asia."† This is undoubtedly true. Next to the Jews, the Armenians will form the most generally useful body of christian missionaries.

* This institution not only assists occasionally, but pensions permanently Europeans, Mahomedans, and Hindoos.

† Fabricii Lux Evangelii, p. 651.

They are to be found in every principal city of Asia; they are the general merchants of the east, and are in a state of constant motion from Canton to Constantinople. Their general character is that of a wealthy, industrious, and enterprising people. They are settled in all the principal places of India, where they arrived many centuries before the English. Wherever they colonize, they build churches, and observe the solemnities of the christian religion in a decorous manner. Their ecclesiastical establishment in Hindostan is more respectable than that of the English. Like us, they have *three* churches in the three capitals, one at Calcutta, one at Madras, and one at Bombay; but they have also churches in the interior of the country.* The bishop sometimes visits Calcutta; but he is not resident there. The proper country of these christians is Armenia, the greater part of which is subject to the Persian government; but they are scattered all over the empire, the commerce of Persia being chiefly conducted by Armenians. Their patriarch resides at *Erivan,* not far from Mount *Ararat*.

The history of the Armenian church is very interesting. Of all the christians in central Asia, they have preserved themselves most free from Mahomedan and Papal corruptions. The pope assailed them for a time with great violence, but with little effect. The churches in lesser Armenia indeed consented to an union, which did not long continue; but those in Persian Armenia maintained their independence; and they retain their ancient scriptures, doctrines, and worship, to this day. "It is marvellous," says an intelligent traveller, who was much among them, "how the Armenian christians have preserved their faith, equally against the vexatious oppression of the Mahomedans their sovereigns, and against the persuasions of the Romish church, which for more than two centuries has endeavoured, by missionaries, priests, and monks, to attach them to her communion. It is impossible to describe the artifices and expenses of the court of Rome to effect this object; but all in vain."†

The Bible was translated into the Armenian language in the fifth century, under very auspicious circumstances,

* In Bengal alone, they have churches at Dacca, Sydabad, and Chinsurah.
† Cardin, vol. II. p. 232.

the history of which has come down to us. It has been allowed, by competent judges of the language, to be a most faithful translation. La Croze calls it "the queen of versions."* This Bible has ever remained in the possession of the Armenian people; and many illustrious instances of genuine and enlightened piety occur in their history. The manuscript copies not being sufficient for the demand, a council of Armenian bishops assembled in 1662, and resolved to call in aid the art of printing, of which they had heard in Europe. For this purpose they applied first to France, but the catholic church refused to print their Bible. At length it was printed at Amsterdam in 1666, and afterwards two other editions in 1668 and 1698. Since that time it has been printed at Venice. One of the editions, which the author has seen, is not inferior, in beauty of typography, to the best English Bible. How far these editions might have supplied the churches in Persia at that time, he does not know; but, at present, the Armenian scriptures are very rare in that country, bearing no proportion to the Armenian population; and, in India, a copy is scarcely to be purchased at any price.

The Armenians in Hindostan are our own subjects. They acknowledge our government in India, as they do that of the Sophi in Persia; and they are entitled to our regard. They have preserved the Bible in its purity; and their doctrines are, as far as the author knows, the doctrines of the Bible. Besides, they maintain the solemn observance of christian worship, throughout our empire, on the seventh day; and they have as many spires pointing to heaven among the Hindoos, as we ourselves. Are such a people then entitled to no acknowledgement on our part, as fellow-christians? Are they for ever to be ranked by us with Jews, Mahomedans, and Hindoos?† Would it not become us to approach nearer to these our subjects, endeavour to gain

* Mr. Joannes Lassar, who is now making a version of the scriptures in the Chinese language in Bengal, is an Armenian christian, and translates chiefly from the Armenian Bible. But he also understands English, and consults the English version.

† Sarkies Joannes, an Armenian merchant of Calcutta, when he heard of the king's recovery from illness in 1789, liberated all the prisoners for debt in the gaol of Calcutta. His majesty, hearing of this instance of loyalty in an Armenian subject, sent him his picture in miniature. Sarkies wore the royal present suspended at his breast, during his life; and it is now worn by his son, when he appears at the levee of the governor-general.

M 2

their confidence, and conciliate their esteem? Let us, at least, do that which is easily practicable. We are in possession of the means of *printing*, which they have not. Let us print the Armenian Bible, and employ proper persons from among themselves, to superintend the work, and encourage them to disperse their own faithful copy throughout the east. Let us show them, that the diffusion of the scriptures is an undertaking to which we are not indifferent; and, by our example, let us stimulate their zeal, which is very languid. But, however languid their zeal may be, it is certain that they consider the English as being yet more dead to the interests of religion, than themselves. Such a subject as this, indeed every subject which is of great importance to christianity, is worthy the notice of our government, as well as of individuals and societies. The printing press, which shall be employed in multiplying copies of the pure Armenian Bible, will prove a precious fountain for the evangelization of the east; and the Oriental Bible repository at Calcutta will be a central and convenient place for its dispersion.

ECCLESIASTICAL ESTABLISHMENT FOR BRITISH INDIA.

BEFORE the auther left India, he published a "Memoir of the expediency of an ecclesiastical establishment" for our empire in the east. The design of that work was first suggested to him by the Rev. Dr. Porteus, late bishop of London, who had attentively surveyed the state of our dominions in Asia; and he was encouraged by subsequent communications with the Marquis Wellesley, to endeavour to lead the attention of the nation to the subject. That publication has now been four years before the public; and many volumes have been written on the various subjects which it contains: but he does not know that any objection has been made to the principle of an ecclesiastical establishment for christians in India. An attempt has been made indeed to divert the attention from the true object, and, instead of considering it as an establishment for christians, to set it forth as an establishment for instructing the Hindoos. But the instruction of the Hindoos is entirely a distinct consideration, as was carefully noted in the memoir. At the end of the first part is the following paragraph:—

"It will be remembered, that nothing which has been observed is intended to imply that any peculiar provision should be made immediately for the instruction of the natives. Any expensive establishment of this kind, however becoming our national character, or obligatory on our principles, cannot possibly be organized to efficient purpose, without the aid of a *local* church. Let us first establish our own religion amongst *ourselves*, and our Asiatic subjects will soon benefit by it. When once our national church shall have been confirmed in India, the members of that church will be the best qualified to advise the state, as to the means by which, from time to time, the civilization of the natives may be promoted."*

An ecclesiastical establishment would yet be necessary for British India, *if there were not a Mahomedan or Hindoo in the land.* For, besides the thousands of British christians, who live and die in that country, there are hundreds of thousands of native christians, who are at this moment "as sheep without a shepherd;" and who are not insensible to their destitute estate, but supplicate our countenance and protection. Surely the measure cannot be contemplated by the legislature, for a moment, without perceiving its absolute propriety, on the common principles of justice and humanity.

In regard to the other subject, the instruction of the Hindoos, many different opinions have been delivered in the volumes alluded to, the most prominent of which are the two following: First, that Hinduism is, upon the whole, as good as christianity, and that therefore conversion to christianity is not necessary. This deserves no reply. The second opinion is, that it is indeed a sacred duty to convert the Hindoos, but that we must not do it by force. With this opinion the author perfectly coincides. To convert men by any other means than those of persuasion, is a practice fit only for the inquisition, and com-

* Memoir, p. 20.

pletely at variance with the tenor of every page which he has written. The means of conversion, which he has recommended, are those which are appointed in the holy scriptures, namely, "Preaching, and the word of God." The first and present means are the translation of the word of God into the various languages; and the next are the labours of teachers and preachers.

The author is not, nor has he ever been, the advocate for force and personal injury toward the Hindoos. No: he pleads the cause of humanity. The object of his work, and of his researches, has been to deliver the people of Hindostan from painful and sanguinary rites; to rescue the devoted victim from the wheels of Moloch's tower; to snatch the tender infant from the jaws of the alligator; to save the aged parent from premature death in the Ganges; to extinguish the flames of the female sacrifice, and to "cause the widow's heart to sing for joy."

Another object of his work has been, to show, that while the feelings of the christian are painfully affected by the exhibition of these sufferings and atrocities, infidelity, on the other hand, can behold them, and DOES behold them, with all the coldness and apathy of Voltaire. And this is the great practical triumph of christianity over philosophical unbelief. While by the former, the best feelings of our nature are meliorated, and improved, and softened, and extended; they become, by the influence of the latter, sullen, and cold, and torpid, and dead.

The remaining opinion on this subject, which is worthy of notice, is the following: "The conversion of the Hindoos to christianity is indeed a solemn obligation, if practicable; but the attempt may possibly displease the Hindoos and endanger our empire." This fear is grounded solely on an ignorance of facts, and on the remoteness of the scene. Christianity began to be preached to Hindoos by Europeans, 300 years ago, and whole provinces are now covered with christians. In the present endeavours of protestant missionaries, the chief difficulty which they generally experience is to awaken the mind of the torpid Hindoos to the subject. They know that every man may choose the religion he likes best, and profess it with impunity; that he may lose his cast and buy a cast again, as he buys an article of merchandize.

There are a hundred casts of religion in Hindostan; and there is no common interest about a particular religion. When one native meets another on the road, he seldom expects to find that he is of the same cast with himself. They are a divided people. Hindostan is like the great world in miniature; when you pass a great river or lofty mountain, you generally find a new variety. Some persons in Europe think it must be a novelty to the Hindoos to see a missionary. There have been for ages past, numerous casts of missionaries in Hindostan, Pagan, Mahomedan, and Christian, all seeking to porselyte individuals to a new religion, or to some new sect of an old one. The difficulty, as the author has already observed, in regard to the protestant teachers, is to awaken attention to *their* doctrine.

The general indifference of the natives to these attempts, whether successful or not, has been demonstrated by recent events. After the adversaries of christian missions had circulated their pamphlets through British India, with the best intention no doubt, according to their judgment, announcing the intelligence that some of the English wanted to convert the inhabitants by force, and to set Hindostan in flames; the natives seem to have considered the information as absurd or unintelligible, and to have treated it with contempt. For immediately afterwards, when, by the defection of the British troops, the foundations of our empire were shaken to their centre, both Mahomedans and Hindoos (who, if they wished to rebel, needed only to sound that trumpet which was first sounded by a senior merchant in Leadenhall Street, no doubt with the best intentions) evinced their accustomed loyalty, and crowded round the standard of the supreme government in the hour of danger.*

There is one argument for the expediency of an ecclesiastical establishment, which the author did not insist

* A worthy clergyman belonging to the presidency of Fort St. George, who witnessed the troops marching against each other, and knew not for a time, what would be the fate of the empire; after the danger was over, makes the following most just and striking reflection, in a letter to a friend. "It cannot but have occurred to every reflecting mind, in looking back on past scenes, if it had pleased God in his providence to have dispossessed us of our dominions, how little would have remained to show, that a people blessed with the light of the glorious gospel of Christ, had once born sway in this land! But now," (he adds exultingly, in allusion to the translation of the scriptures) "the word of God in the languages of all India, will be an enduring MONUMENT of British piety and liberality, for which the sacrifice of prayer and thanksgiving will ascend to the Most High, to the latest generations."

on strongly in the memoir, from motives of delicacy; but recent events have rendered the same reserve no longer necessary. He will proceed therefore to disclose a fact, which will serve to place the motives for recommending such an establishment, in their just light. It is not the giving the christian religion to the natives which will endanger our empire, but the *want of religion among our own countrymen.* After the disturbance among the British officers in Bengal in 1794, which for a time had a most alarming aspect, being of the same character with that which took place lately at Madras, a memorial was presented to the Marquis Wellesley, on his accession to the government, by persons who had been long in the service of the company, and were well acquainted with the circumstances of the empire at large; representing the necessity of a suitable "*religious establishment* for British India," and illustrating that necessity by the events which had recently taken place in the army. That memorial referred to the almost total extinction of christian worship, at the military stations, where the seventh day was only distinguished by the British flag; and noticed the fatal consequences that might be expected from large bodies of men, far remote from the controlling power of the parent state, enjoying luxury and independence, and seeing nothing, from youth to age, of the religion of their country. It showed further, that, of the whole number of English who go to India, not a *tenth* part return; and assigned this fact as a reason why their religion should follow them to the east; that it might be, in the first place, a solace to themselves, in the dreary prospect of dying in that land (for of a thousand soldiers in sickly India, there will be generally a hundred in declining health) and secondly, "that it might be some security for their loyalty to their king, and their attachment to the principles of their country."

It required not a memorial to apprise Marquis Wellesley of the truth of these facts, or of the justness of the reasoning upon them. The necessity of a meliorated state of society for the English armies, was made evident to him by his own observation; and it cannot be doubted that, had that nobleman remained in India, to complete the plans he meditated for the advantage of that country, and had his coadjutor, Mr. Pitt, lived, a suitable religious establishment would have been, by this time, proposed to the East India company, for every part of their dominions in Hindostan. But Marquis Wellesley had another and a more imperious service first to perform, and this was, to SAVE THE BODY OF THE EMPIRE ITSELF. British Hindostan was, at that moment, surrounded by strong and formidable enemies, who were putting themselves "in the attitude of the tiger," as a Vakeel of Tippoo expressed it, "to leap upon the prey." And this service that great statesman achieved under divine providence, first, by destroying the Mysorean empire, under Tippoo Sultaun, and thereby extinguishing the Mahomedan power in Hindostan; secondly, by overwhelming the hitherto invincible Mahrattas; and lastly, by forming on the frontier a league of strength, which like *a wall of iron*, has saved the country from native invasion ever since; notwithstanding its subsequent critical and exposed state, in consequence of frequent changes of the supreme government, and of dissensions in our army. The services which that nobleman performed for our empire in the east were very ill understood at the time: his views were so comprehensive, that few men could embrace them. They are more generally acknowledged now; but it is to be apprehended that some years must yet elapse, before all the beneficial consequences of his administration, will be fully made known to his country.

It has been a subject of wonder to many in England, that our army should at any time betray symptoms of disaffection in India, when no instance of it occurs elsewhere. But the surprise will cease, when the circumstances before mentioned shall have been duly weighed. Of the individuals engaged in the late disturbances at Madras, there were perhaps some, who had not witnessed the service of christian worship for twenty years; whose minds were impressed by the daily view of the rites of the Hindoo religion, and had lost almost all memory of their own. It is morally impossible to live long in such circumstances, without being in some degree affected by them. That loyalty is but little to be depended on, whether abroad or at home, which has lost the basis of religion.

The true spring of the irregular proceedings, contemptuous remonstrance, and ultimate disaffection of the military in India, is this; large bodies of troops at a great distance from Britain, which they never expect to see again, begin, after a long absence, to feel more sensibly their own independence, while their affection for their native country gradually diminishes. And if, under such circumstances, they have not the restraints of religion, (for what is obedience "to the powers that be" but the restraint of religion?) and if they have not the frequent view of christian worship to recal their minds, by association of ideas, to the sacred ordinances and principles of their country, it is impossible to foresee to what degrees of rebellion or infatuation they may proceed. It is unjust to ascribe these proceedings to the casual acts of the governor for the time being. Indiscreet measures on his part may form the pretext; but the true cause lies much deeper. The company's officers in India are as honourable a body of military men as are to be found in the world, the author knows them, but they are in peculiar circumstances; and if any other description of troops were in their stead, passing a whole life in such an *unchristianizing* service, the same causes would still produce the same effects.

The most alarming consideration, while things remain in their present state, is this, that, in proportion as our empire increases, and our force in India grows stronger, the danger arising from the foregoing causes, becomes the greater. These are obvious truths, on which it is not necessary to dilate. But there is another subject allied to this, which the author thinks it a solemn duty to bring before the public.

Not only are our troops denied suitable religious instruction, when they arrive in India, but they are destitute of it, *during their long voyage* to that country. The voyage is, on an average, six months. Now, provision ought certainly to be made for divine worship, and for spiritual consolation to the soldiers, during that period; for it is sometimes a period of great sickness, and of frequent death. Indeed there ought to be a chaplain on board of every India ship.*

* The East India company require the commander or purser of every ship to read prayers on Sunday, when the weather permits. The service is performed,

They who profess to believe in the christian religion, ought also to believe in the superintending providence of God; ought to believe that the divine blessing will accompany those designs which are undertaken in his name, and conducted in his fear. If we were a heathen nation, then might we send forth our fleets without a prayer, and commit them, for a safe voyage, "to goddess Fortune and fair winds." But we are a christian nation, though not a superstitious one; and, however individuals may consider it, it is certain that our countrymen in general, view the performance of the offices of religion with great respect; and that, in particular circumstances on board ship, no duty is more acceptable, none more interesting, none more salutary and consoling. Such scenes the author himself has witnessed; and from those persons who have witnessed such scenes, he has never heard but one opinion as to the propriety of having a clergyman to form one of the great family in a ship, in these long, sickly, and perilous voyages. When the news arrived in England last year of the loss of the seven Indiamen in a distant ocean, how gratifying would it have been to surviving friends, if they could have been assured that the offices of religion and the consolations of its ministers, had been afforded to those who perished, during their last days!* These events have a warning voice; and it is not unbecoming a great and respectable body of men, like the East India company, to attend to it. The author has already remarked, that the legislature has not neglected a subject of this importance. It is required that

in many cases, in a serious and truly impressive manner; and the acknowledged good effects in such cases, convey the strongest recommendation of the measure which has been proposed. One important duty of the chaplain of an Indiaman might be to superintend the studies of the young writers and cadets proceeding to India; who, for want of some direction of this kind, generally pass the long voyage in idleness, lounging on the quarter deck, or gambling in the cuddy. So important has this subject been considered, that during the administration of Marquis Wellesley, a detailed plan for carrying the proposed measure into effect was actually transmitted to a member of the court of directors, to lay before the court. If it were made an indispensable qualification of the chaplain, that he should understand the rudiments of the Persian and Hindostanee languages, and the common elements of geometry and navigation, for the instruction of the midshipmen, his services would be truly important, merely in his secular character. Every truly respectable commander in the company's service, must be happy to have an exemplary clergyman on board his ship.

* The Rev. Paul Limrick was a passenger on board one of these ships. Mr. Limrick was second chaplain at the presidency of Fort-William; an amiable, benevolent and respectable man, whose loss will be heard of with deep regret by a large body of the inhabitants of Calcutta, and of his friends in Europe.

every ship of the line should have a chaplain; and we have lately seen some of our most renowned admirals, both before and after battle, causing the prayers and thanksgivings of the fleet to ascend to the God of heaven.

There still remains one topic more, to which the author would advert. It may be presumed to be the wish of the major part of this nation, that whenever a missionary of exemplary character and of respectable recommendation, applies to the East India company for a passage to our eastern shores, his request might be treated with indulgence. In him we export a blessing (as he may prove to be) to thousands of our fellow-creatures; and his example, and instructions, and prayers will do no harm to the ship in which he sails. While the East India company retain the sole privilege of conveyance to India, the nation would be pleased to see this condescension shown to persons in humble circumstances, whose designs are of a public character, and acknowledged by all men to be pious and praiseworthy. The author will conclude these observations with a paragraph which he has found in a manuscript of the Rev. Mr. Kohloff of Tanjore, the successor of Mr. Swartz, which has been just transmitted for publication:—

"It is a remarkable fact, that since the foundation of our mission, which is now one hundred years, and during which period upwards of fifty missionaries have arrived from Europe; among the many ships that have been lost, there never perished one vessel, WHICH HAD A MISSIONARY ON BOARD."*

The following letter, written by Dr. WATSON, bishop of Llandaff, on the subject of an ecclesiastical establishment for British India, was published in Calcutta, in the year 1807.

"*Calgarth Park, Kendale,*
14*th May*, 1806.

"REVEREND SIR,

"Some weeks ago I received your MEMOIR of the expediency of an ecclesiastical establishment for British India; for which obliging attention I now return you my best thanks. I hesitated for some time whether I ought

* MS. materials for the Life of Swartz.

to interrupt your speculations with my acknowledgements for so valuable a present; but on being informed of the noble premium, by which you propose to exercise the talents of graduates in the university of Cambridge, I determined to express to you my admiration of your disinterestedness, and zeal in the cause of christianity.

"Twenty years and more have now elapsed since, in a sermon, before the house of lords, I hinted to the then government, the propriety of paying regard to the propagation of christianity in India; and I have since then, as fit occasions offered, privately, but unsuccessfully, pressed the matter on the consideration of those in power. If my voice or opinion can, in future, be of any weight with the king's ministers, I shall be most ready to exert myself, in forwarding any prudent measure for promoting a liberal ecclesiastical establishment in British India; it is not without consideration that I say a liberal establishment, because I heartily wish that every christian should be at liberty to worship God according to his conscience, and be assisted therein by a teacher, at the public expense, of his own persuasion.

"The subjects you have proposed for the work which shall obtain your prize, are all of them judiciously chosen, and if properly treated (as my love for my Alma Mater persuades me they will be) may probably turn the thoughts of the legislature towards the measure you recommend.

"The *Salutaris Lux Evangelii*, by Fabricius, published at Hamburg in 1731, will be of great use to the candidates for your prize; and his *Index Geographicus* EPISCOPATUUM *Orbis Christiani*, subjoined to that work, might, if accompanied with proper notes, afford a very satisfactory elucidation of your third head.

"God in his providence, hath so ordered things, that America, which three hundred years ago was peopled by none but Pagans, has now many millions of christians in it; and will not, probably, three hundred years hence, have a single Pagan in it, but be occupied by more christians, and more enlightened christians than now exist in Europe.

"Africa is not now worse fitted for the reception of christianity than America was, when it was first visited by Europeans; and Asia is much better fitted for it, in as much as Asia enjoys a considerable degree of civilization; and some degree of it is necessary to the successful introduction of christianity. The commerce and colonization of christian states have civilized America, and they will, in process of time, civilize and christianize the whole earth. Whether it be a christian duty to attempt, by lenient methods, to propagate the christian religion among Pagans and Mahomedans, can be doubted, I think, by few; but whether any attempt will be attended with much success, till christianity is purified from its corruptions, and the lives of christians are rendered correspondent to their christian profession, may be doubted by many; but there certainly never was a more promising opportunity of trying the experiment of subverting Paganism in India, than that which has for some years been offered to the government of Great Britain.

"The morality of our holy religion is so salutary to civil society, its promises of a future state so consolatory to individuals, its precepts so suited to the deductions of the most improved reason, that it must finally prevail throughout the world. Some have thought that christianity is losing ground in christendom. I am of a different opinion. Some ascititious doctrines, derived from Rome and Geneva, are losing ground amongst learned men; some unchristian practices springing from ignorance, bigotry, intolerance, self-sufficiency of opinion, with uncharitableness of judgment, are losing ground among all sober-minded men; but a belief in Jesus Christ, as the Saviour of the world, as the medium through whom eternal life will be given to all who obey his gospel, is more and more confirmed every day in the minds of men of eminence and erudition, not only in this, but in every other christian country. From this praise I am not disposed to exclude even France itself, notwithstanding the temporary apostacy of some of its philosophers from every degree of religious faith. I cannot but hope well of that country, when I see its national institute proposing for public discussion the following subject; 'What has been the influence of the reformation of Luther, on the political situation of the different states of Europe, and on the progress of knowledge?' especially when I see the subject treated by Mr. Villers, in a manner which would have derived honour to the most liberal protestant in the freest state in Europe.

"It is not to be denied, that the morals of christians in general fall far short of the standard of christian perfection, and have ever done so, scarcely excepting the latter end of the first century. Yet, notwithstanding this concession, it is a certain fact, that the christian religion has always operated to the production of piety, benevolence, self-government, and the love of virtue amongst individuals, in every country where it has been received; and it will every where operate more powerfully, as it is received with more firm assurance of its truth; and it will be every where received with more firm assurance of its truth, as it is better understood; for when it is properly understood, it will be freed from the pollutions of superstition and fanaticism among the hearers, and from ambition, domination and secularity among the teachers.

"Your publication has given us in England a great insight into the state of christianity in India, as well as into the general state of learning amongst you; and it has excited in me the warmest wishes for the prosperity of the college of Fort-William. It is an institution which would have done honour to the wisdom of Solon or Lycurgus. I have no knowledge personally of the Marquis Wellesley, but I shall think of him and of his coadjutors in this undertaking, with the highest respect and admiration, as long as I live.

"I cannot enter into any particulars relative to an ecclesiastical establishment in India; nor would it, perhaps, be proper to press government to take the matter into their consideration, till this country is freed from the danger which threatens it; but I have that opinion of his majesty's ministers, that they will, not only from policy, but from a serious sense of religious duty, be disposed to treat the subject, whenever it comes before them, with great judgment and liberality. May God direct their counsels!

"'Our empire in India,' said Mr. Hastings, 'has been acquired by the sword, and must be maintained by the sword.' I cannot agree with him in this sentiment. All empires have been originally acquired by violence, but they are best established by moderation and justice.

There was a time when we showed ourselves to the inhabitants of India in the character of tyrants and robbers; that time, I trust, is gone for ever. The wisdom of British policy, the equity of its jurisprudence, the impartiality of its laws, the humanity of its penal code, and above all, the incorrupt administration of public justice, will, when they are well understood, make the Indians our willing subjects, and induce them to adopt a religion attended with such consequences to the dearest interests of the human mind. They will rejoice in having exchanged the tyranny of pagan superstition, and the despotism of their native princes, for the mild mandates of christianity, and the stable authority of equitable laws. The difference between such different states of civil society, as to the production of human happiness, is infinite; and the attainment of happiness is the ultimate aim of all individuals in all nations.

I am, reverend Sir,
Your obliged and faithful servant,
R. LLANDAFF."

To Rev. Dr. Buchanan,
Vice-Provost of the College of Fort-William, Calcutta.

CONCLUSION.

In the progress of these researches the author has found his mind frequently drawn to consider the extraordinary difference of opinion, which exists among men of learning, in regard to the importance and obligation of communicating religious knowledge to our fellow-creatures. And he has often heard the question asked by others, What can be the cause of this discrepancy of opinion? For that such a difference does exist is most evident; and is exemplified at this moment in some of the most illustrious characters for rank and learning, in the nation. This is a problem of a very interesting character at this day, and worthy of a distinct and ample discussion, particularly at the seats of learning. The problem may be thus expressed: "What power is that, which produces in the minds of some persons a real interest and concern in the welfare of their fellow-creatures; extending not only to the comfort of their existence in this world, but to their felicity hereafter; while other men who are apparently in similar circumstances as to learning and information, do not feel inclined to *move one step* for the promotion of such objects?"—The latter, it may be, can speculate on the philosophy of the human mind, on its great powers and high dignity, on the sublime virtue of universal benevolence, on the tyranny of superstition, and the slavery of ignorance; and will sometimes quote the verse of the poet,

"Homo sum: humani nil a me alienum puto:"

but they leave it to others, and generally to the christian in humble life, to exercise the spirit of that noble verse. This is a very difficult problem; and it has been alleged by some that it cannot be solved on any known principles of philosophy. The following relation will probably lead to principles by which we may arrive at a solution.

There was once a king in the east, whose empire extended over the known world, and his dominion "was to the end of the earth." During the former part of his reign, his heart was filled with pride: he knew not the God of heaven: and he viewed with the utmost indifference the nations over whom he ruled, worshipping idols of wood and stone. But it pleased the King of kings to dethrone this haughty monarch, to cast him down from his high estate, and to abase him in the dust. And after he had been for a time in the furnace of affliction, and his proud heart was humbled, God graciously revealed himself to him in his true name and character, and then restored him to his former prosperity and power. The penitent king, thus once more exalted, and filled with admiration at the discovery of the ONLY TRUE GOD, immediately issued an edict to the whole world, setting forth the greatness of the Most High, asserting his glory, and inviting all nations to "praise and magnify HIM that liveth for ever, whose dominion is an everlasting dominion, and his kingdom is from generation to generation." This memorable edict began in these sublime terms:—

"NEBUCHADNEZZAR THE KING, UNTO ALL PEOPLE, NATIONS, AND LANGUAGES, THAT DWELL IN ALL THE EARTH, Peace be multiplied unto you. I thought it good to shew the signs and wonders which the Most

High God hath wrought toward me. How great are his SIGNS! How mighty are his WONDERS!" Having recounted the judgment and mercy of God to himself, he thus concludes; "Now I Nebuchadnezzar, praise and extol and honour the King of Heaven, all whose works are truth and his ways judgment; and them that walk in pride he is able to abase."*

Such a proclamation to the nations of the earth was a noble act of a king, and ought to be had in perpetual remembrance. It reminds us of the last charge of HIM "who ascended up on high:" Go, TEACH ALL NATIONS. It discovers to us the new and extended benevolence, greatness of mind, and pure and heavenly charity, which distinguish that man, whose heart has been impressed by THE GRACE OF GOD. How solemn his sense of duty! How ardent to declare the glory of his Saviour! His views for the good of men, how disinterested and enlarged!—It is but too evident, that all our speculations concerning a divine revelation, and the obligation imposed on us to study it ourselves, or to communicate it to others, are cold and uninteresting, and excite not to action, "until, through the tender compassion of God, the Day-spring from on high visit us, to give light to them that sit in darkness;"† to humble our hearts, at the remembrance of our sins against God, and to affect them with a just admiration of his pardoning mercy.

Let Great Britain imitate the example of the Chaldean king; and send forth to all the world, her TESTIMONY concerning the True God. She also reigns over many nations which "worship idols of wood and stone;" and she ought, in like manner, to declare to them "the SIGNS and WONDERS of the Almighty." And, in this design, every individual will concur, of every church, family, and name, whose heart has been penetrated with just apprehensions of the Most High God; having known his judgments and experienced his mercy.

* Daniel, 4th chapter. † Luke ii. 79.

THE END.

Kirby Hall, Boroughbridge,
Feb. 15, 1811.

W. KELLY, LIVERPOOL.